# Give Me This Mountain

*Helen Roseveare*

CHRISTIAN
FOCUS

Copyright © Helen Roseveare 2006

paperback ISBN 978-1-84550-189-1
epub ISBN 978-1-84550-934-7
mobi ISBN 978-1-84550-935-4

10  9  8  7  6

*Give Me This Mountain*
First published in 1966
This edition published in 2006
Reprinted in 2007, 2010, 2012, 2016 & 2017
by
Christian Focus Publications,
Geanies House, Fearn, Ross-shire,
IV20 1TW, Scotland, UK

www.christianfocus.com

Cover design by Moose77.com

Printed and bound by
Bell & Bain, Glasgow

# Contents

And Caleb said: Now therefore give me this mountain, whereof the Lord spake in that day; for thou heardest in that day how the Anakims were there, and that the cities were great and fenced: if so be the lord will be with me, then I shall be able to drive them out, as the Lord said. And Joshua gave unto Caleb Hebron for an inheritance.

Joshua 14:12–13

# Foreword

In 1989, around 120 young people sat cross-legged in the Piper living room and dining room, covering nearly every square inch of floor space. They had accepted our open invitation to anyone who thought missions might be in his or her future. I wish I could remember more of what Dr. Helen Roseveare told us that evening. But part of her message might easily have been the heart of this book, *Give Me this Mountain*: "I believe that, at its simplest, a missionary is one sent by God to live a Christian life, usually amongst people other than his own. It is *living* which counts. This may include formal preaching, but it will certainly include personal relationships, and these often have to be worked out under most trying conditions." That reminds me of what Jim Elliot is supposed to have said about missionaries, "They're just a bunch of nobodies trying to exalt Somebody. In fact, they're pretty much the same kind of folks as you and your family."

The main reason I keep coming back to Helen's books is her unembarrassed forthrightness in portraying her normal, weak, and self-centered seasons. I can hardly imagine letting the world into my life as she does. Her experience to helps me realize that, as she says about herself, I cannot "escape from myself by going to Congo [or whatever my escape route might be]. Rather, I came to know myself better, perhaps more as others had already seen me." Each time I read one of her accounts, I want to be like her, I want to know God as she does.

In sensitive contrast to that candor is her understated reserve in recounting stories of her bravery and faith that reflect God's witness to himself during the terrifying, deadly days of the Simba Revolt.

Her stories are about a real person with a real God. And the the exultant end of so many of her stories is the great release and relief of once again being still and knowing that *God* is God and I'm not.

Noël Piper
Minneapolis, Minnesota
Author of *Faithful Women and Their Extraordinary God*

# Introduction

In the following pages I have tried to write an honest, unadorned story of my somewhat tempestuous life. Except in the Epilogue I have not tried to draw any morals. But neither have I wanted to pull any punches. I have tried honestly to thank those who have helped me along the way and to be careful not to criticize unkindly others with whom I disagreed. At times this may have made the story a little lopsided since occasionally I have felt unable to give publicly all the facts that influenced me at certain periods. I do not think, however, that this materially alters the basic story.

I have only once in my life kept a diary, and that was under the special stress of the five months in rebel captivity from August to December, 1964. All the rest of the story comes as my memory prompts me. There may be some chronological discrepancies. Many episodes are excluded, either because they have been forgotten or else because I did not consider that they helped forward the main theme. Other episodes are mentioned and then never referred to again. They were there, but did not substantially alter the course of the journey.

My life has possibly included more dramatic episodes than many another, but this is not the impression I wish to leave with any reader. Rather, it has been for me a journey towards one definite and glorious goal, 'that I may know him...', our God, revealed to us in his Son, the Lord Jesus Christ. I have often felt that my life was akin to mountaineering, with a clear goal to reach the highest peak. There may be a fairly long journey to reach the foothills before the real climb begins. On the way up, clouds or lesser peaks often hide the goal from view, but the original sight of the summit keeps us pressing on, despite weariness and even discouragement.

I found frequently that I climbed in glorious sunshine, warm and invigorating, my face set determinedly for the nearest peak I could see. As I reached it, I revelled in the sense of achievement and victory and in the glorious view. I did all I could to encourage others to join me and to help them up over the difficult parts. Then, slowly, my imagination would be caught by the next peak ahead, higher, steeper, but again bathed in sunlight, and eventually the resolve would form to set off upwards again.

Here I made a mistake, many times, as the story shows. As I went down from the present peak into the valley between the mountains, I was often shadowed by the very peak I had been enjoying. This I interpreted in a sense of failure and this often led to despair. I felt I was going down into the 'slough of despond'. I see now that I was wrong in this 'feeling'. The going down was merely an initial moving forward towards the next higher ground, never a going back to base level. The shadow was only relative after the brightness of the sun; the valley could provide rest for working out the experiences previously learnt, a time for refreshment before the next hard climb. Had I understood this meaning of the sunshine and shadow in my life rather than interpreting my experiences along life's way as 'up' and 'down', I might have saved myself many deep heartaches.

I trust, despite this failure, that readers will be able to enter into the joy of this wonderful pilgrimage and the satisfaction of a life spent seeking to know the One who alone gives life. I am in no way offering my story as an example for others to follow. There are many mistakes that I hope may warn others. There are streaks in my nature that I am glad to see the Lord is dealing with, and I should hate others to think that they ought to emulate them. I think especially of the tremendous ambition to be a success in anything I undertook, which so often drove me to set myself standards which, under all the circumstances, were not required and which, if I had been more perceptive, I should have known I had no chance of achieving. No, it is not an example; but maybe it will be an

# 1

# Getting to the Start

'Either you join us, or you go down by yourself: it's your own affair.'

The nursemaid moved away. I swallowed hard, my eyes misting with tears. Five minutes before everything had been so different as I had run and scrambled up the wooded pathway with my elder brother, gathering wild flowers, happy in the flickering sunlight, chattering and unconcerned. I had noticed Bob's face set in a quiet determination and had wondered. Then we came out from the trees at the top of the ghyll and stood on the flat rock overlooking the rushing stream, silenced, as always, by the noise of the waters and a sense of power and awe at its depth. Suddenly, quietly, so unexpectedly, Bob drew back a few paces, ran and jumped the ghyll. My eyes followed him with silent admiration, and yet with horror glancing down at the fury below. He had done it—our much-discussed exploit of jumping the raging torrent from the rock. Determinedly I drew back, clenched my fists, closed my eyes, ran up to it and stopped dead!

Bob had run on into the woods, suddenly a man, alone, successful. Then the nursemaid struggled up, carrying my four-year-old younger sister. She stepped over the narrow channel with one easy stride, and told me to hurry up and join them; they couldn't wait all day. Then she moved on, to follow Bob down the pathway the other side.

Despair, loneliness, tears, I could not do what Bob had done, and jump across. The more I longed, the greater the noise and depth and width and horror. I was terrified of that water. With a wild sense of defeat, I turned and rushed back down the hill, burning tears of shame choking me. What would he think? Would he play with me again? I was just a sissy, a girl, afraid—yes, that was it—afraid of water and heights.

This longing to be accepted, this need to be loved, to be wanted, so often a part of childhood, came early to me. There was that day in Cornwall two years before, when suddenly a hush fell on the crowded beach, and Mother noticed all eyes being drawn in one direction. Way up the sheer face of the cliff on a narrow ledge, unable to go up or down, she saw the round, diminutive figure of her four-year-old, trying to defeat this sense of inferiority, longing to shine in the eyes of her adored six-year-old brother.

As a child I was endlessly active, restless with animal spirits, always in mischief, with an urge to excel, to be noticed, to be the centre of the group, an inner need to be admired—and life often seemed very hard and unsympathetic. Often blamed for trouble that was not of my making, I would despise the others in my heart for not owning up to clear me of the accusation.

School soon absorbed much of my excess energy, but the work came easily. Books were a fascination, so much so that, when my younger sister whispered, 'Read to me, Peggy', in the dark of an evening, I could forget the whipping I had earlier suffered unjustly. Lying side by side, by torch light, under the blankets, we devoured many of the thrills of Long John Silver, the White Rabbit, Pooh and Henry Esmond, and the world took on new silvery lights of happiness and mystery.

This air of mystery laid the foundation of Sundays. I loved this day and the sense of difference—dressed tidily, walking up the steep, narrow road past the curio shop, where two white stone cherub bookends smiled at me each Sunday as I ran ahead of the family, till I had saved enough to make them my mother's birthday present. The cool, dim building, with high, carved wood pews; the thin, tall candles flickering below the amazing coloured east window; the vases of austere white lilies; the choirboys in surplice and ruff, the acolytes and servers, the cross and incense; the priest in his beautifully embroidered linen vestments; the pealing organ and rich strange music that filled the building right up to the great carved dome; the long, difficult words folded into the lilting chants; the sermon with its grave cadences; all these I loved, absorbing almost unconsciously a lasting impression of beauty and solemnity. Then home we would go to a family dinner, so often the only day Dad was with us, and after that off to Sunday school, held locally at the teacher's home. I vividly remember that wonderful day (my eighth birthday) when she talked to us of India, and we cut out pictures of Indian children and stuck them in our 'Missionary Prayer Book'. It was then that the quiet resolve was made. When I grow up, I will go to tell other boys and girls about the Lord Jesus—a child's determination that never faded.

Odd incidents stand out clearly like beacons, all pointing to the absorbing necessity of being loved and wanted. There was the day I had a new dress, in velveteen, plain, dark, with three silver buttons set obliquely each side of the chest, just what I longed for, quite different, smart, commanding. I recall a visit from an American cousin to my school when I was ten and my being sent for by the headmistress who introduced me as 'an exceptional pupil with a brilliant mind'! I had to look up 'exceptional' in a dictionary afterwards, and was very puzzled to know if it was complimentary or not, but it had obviously impressed these important relatives!

The following year, exam-time came round and I woke up feeling ill one morning. Despite it, I struggled to school, starting on a glorious, straightforward maths exam, and then was violently sick after completing only one of the ten questions. I shall never forget the bitter disappointment of having only 10 out of 100 for my best subject, or the subsequent radiant joy when it was not included in the averages and I once again received the form prize for the year. These little things mattered so much.

During these years three memorable summer holidays added to the scenic background of life. The first—through France and Switzerland, then south to Pompeii—had the added joy that my beloved godfather, 'Uncle Ray', accompanied us in his own car. I glowed with happiness at being specially 'his', sometimes travelling on my own with him. The second, with family car and camping equipment, took us through Germany (where we joined the crowds in Berlin to watch the Olympic Games), Hungary (and the Budapest Music festival, with everyone in national costume), Bulgaria (with its back-to-front writing, and nods for nos), to Istanbul (all minarets and tramcars). But it left less impression. The third stands out clear in my memory— the majestic beauty of Norwegian fjords girded by mighty mountains; the deep clear depths; the coastal steamer. Up and on we journeyed through to the far north, where we saw the aurora borealis, splendid in all its magnificence of heavenly colours. There were reindeers and moose; Laplanders, shy and colourful; and the sharp cold of the Arctic. Then back again, through festoons of lakes and stately crimson pines, reflected in glory in the evening sun. Last of all came a few days in Leningrad, travelling by train; guarded by soldiers, sight-seeing by permission!

Then it was my twelfth birthday—and boarding-school. I insisted on changing from my pet name, Peggy, to my real name, Helen. The former now seemed childish, an obstacle to my determination to be a success, to grow up, to be popular. For here at boarding-school, too, the urgent 'need' was to impress, to be loved, to be wanted—a need that grew steadily stronger through these formative years. My vivid imagination found plenty of food for exaggeration in all the experiences of recent holidays, magnifying out of all proportion the happenings and personalities. I boasted of my introduction to Hitler at the Olympic Games in Berlin—weaving truth (that we saw Hitler at the lighting of the torch) and fiction (that I was introduced to him) so cleverly that I myself failed to remember where one ended and the other started. Linked with all this, there was a funny sort of feeling in the back of my mind that I had been sent to boarding-school because I wasn't wanted at home. I do not now think this was true, or fair to my parents; but these are the things that eat their way into a child's mind. It became a must to be popular, to impress; I was hungry to be loved and wanted, yet I just wasn't that type. And so I lied, and magnified still further my fabulous stories. It didn't work. In fact, it had precisely the opposite effect, and I found myself more 'unwanted' than ever.

There were growing needs at other levels too, not least the demands of a quick mind. I found a great urge in me to lead, and there just had to be an outlet for this. Even as a child I could see in a flash a possible line of action—how it could be accomplished—and its consequences! This led me into endless mischief, a scheme for 'escaping from the school block if a fire broke out in the basement cloakroom', for example. Needless to say, the route—through the gymnasium window, across the tiles behind the sewing-room, down a drain-pipe, on to a small flat roof over the music wing—had to be demonstrated; and the severe reprimand that followed when we were found halfway was well merited! I wanted to lead in 'good things', too, but seemed to lack the opportunity and outlet for the healthy, buoyant energy of youth.

Then, again, the urge to learn began to burn in my heart. I would have learnt anything they put in front of me! I longed to grasp knowledge, particularly proven facts, mathematical and scientific, with their orderly reasoning and accurate method. I wasn't, at that stage, interested in the 'end', or the out-working; I just longed to assimilate knowledge for its own sake. With this went a 'need' to win, to dominate, not others, but the facts themselves, to get a 100 per cent not in order to defeat other pupils, but simply for the satisfaction of knowing I had mastered the subject. If I didn't succeed, if I didn't gain the form prize, I'd failed—failed myself. And I probably also felt, deep down, that if I didn't do well I would fail to win the love and respect of my parents and brother, always so deeply important to me.

I joined the school dramatic society. As a youngster at home I had always been fascinated by acting and had organized productions of various plays which were performed in an oasthouse loft with footlights, curtains, stage props and everything else all meticulously correct. The actors were my sisters and any local friends I could inveigle to join us. Proceeds were in aid of mission funds. The school dramatic society, however, was a very different kettle of fish. But still I must be good at everything; I must succeed and be in the limelight. Even though I dreaded every moment of every rehearsal and, when it came to the actual performance, dreaded being in front of people, scared that I would make a fool of myself, yet this inner sense of need drove me on.

Somehow, in the middle of this, I became conscious of God. I've no idea what I thought of God, or who I thought He was; but there was Somebody, God, who was bigger than everything around me, and I needed Him. I needed something big. I needed Someone who was so big He could be bigger than me! And so God came in, and I was confirmed, along with the rest of the Upper IVths. It may not have meant very much. I'm sure I didn't understand the real meaning or full significance of it. But it was a sincere intimation that I realized my need for God. In a stumbling way, it was the conscious start of my search for Him. I had to take hold of this God. Confirmation appeared to be the way people got God, so I was confirmed. God knew, and accepted, and leant towards me to draw me steadily nearer Himself. I wasn't 'converted', it's true. But I'm not sure that God is as interested as we sometimes seem to be in the precise order of the steps that lead to true conversion. At any rate God drew near to me in it all, because He knew that my decision to be confirmed indicated a search for Him, for Someone bigger than myself, Someone I could draw on and depend upon, Someone to deal with all my complicated 'needs', all the complexes and worries that burdened my heart.

Sure enough, shortly afterwards I began to get guilt-stricken about the everlasting troubles I was in—talking in prep., talking in corridors, talking after lights-out—all necessitating a journey to the headmistress on Monday morning. Mounting that dreaded flight of stairs from hall to platform before the assembled school was a weekly affair for me! Not that I was really so much worse than the others. It was just that, when asked, I had to own up. Our school was run on a principle of trust and honour, with no staff supervision, particularly of prep. periods. The form monitor, a girl appointed each term from her own class, was responsible for maintaining discipline. I didn't even need to think when the inevitable question came; I knew perfectly well I must have talked, because I always talked. My great friend Kath and I used to sit together in class. The Monday came when Kath was ill and mine was the only hand that responded to the Form Mistress's 'Anyone talk in prep. on Saturday?' Oh, she said, so you're talking to yourself now, are you? But at break she sent for me, and over a cup of hot milk and a slice of marvellous currant cake in her little study, she had a heart-to-heart talk with me about the stupidity of breaking rules, the value of hard work, and above all, the preciousness of strict honesty. She taught maths, and from then on I was her star pupil!

There was a growing hunger for honesty from this time on. I had to have Someone big enough, above it all, outside, so to speak, who could cope. And I gradually became conscious that I could reach Him only if I were absolutely honest.

At this time, too, came a hunger for beauty. It was wartime, and everything was rather drab—plain white china, blacked-out streets, school uniform clothes, and the tragedy of war. My school was in North Wales, but my home was in Kent. I used to travel through London, and many times saw the blitz, and its awful horrors that, along with the poverty and filth, shocked me bitterly. I remember travelling back to school one day, crossing from south to north London in a bus, when an air raid occurred and panic broke out. Before we could even halt, women leapt from the moving bus, running for shelter in the nearest building. Suddenly a bomb fell on that very house, which crashed in a blazing mass. I watched with horror as Civil Defence men tried to reach the screaming women.

Young though I was, I was deeply upset by the meaning-lessness of it all, feeling that something was fundamentally wrong. Surely Somebody was big enough to get all this into focus. I didn't then know who this Someone was. It was just a search going on inside me for Someone who could cope with all the world's needs, as well as with mine. There was a growing consciousness that everything seemed so useless, so pointless. One went on talking in prep. and reporting to the Head. And on the larger scale, bombs fell and men and women were being killed. Others were hungry and nobody was really bothering to provide them with food. People in other lands had so little, and no-one seemed to care. We read the newspapers, we discussed in school current-events lessons, and through it all was this growing impression that life was meaningless. Where was it all leading? As I tried to probe deeper, I became scared. There was no-one to turn to, no-one to guide one through the rocks.

All this led to an intense reaching out after the Unseen, a developing perfectionist attitude that shrank alike from the sight or sound of destructive suffering, unalleviated poverty, and superficial insincerity. In the summer of 1941 I cycled from school to attend a Society for the Propagation of the Gospel summer school.

Shyness kept me from joining in many of the activities, but I'll never forget the short, daily, devotional sessions led by the chaplain, Father Charles Preston, a 'brown' monk of the Anglican Franciscan order. His face shone with an inner light. His words were always quiet and kindly, never tinged with sarcasm or frivolity, obviously utterly sincere and quietly satisfied. He drew me. He was never hurried or impatient. We sat in the still hush of the chapel and he talked of God, and my heart was filled with longing. Our surroundings melted and he carried me away into the great mysterious Presence of God, and showed me the nail-pierced hands and the out-poured love and the wooing heart of the Saviour.

One evening, with an inexplicable hunger after God, in absolute simplicity and forthright honesty, I made my first 'confession'. An overwhelming sense of release poured into my heart that now God knew all. He knew the very worst about me, and it was now up to Him. The burden of sin and failure and shame rolled away. I went back into the nave of the chapel walking on air. In the dim light, I knelt and read that lovely hymn:

> 'Take my life, and let it be
>  Consecrated, Lord, to Thee …
> Take myself, and I will be
>  Ever, only, all for Thee.'

I meant every word. I walked out quietly into the moonlight, across the grounds, and a great joy flooded my whole being. I felt I could have jumped over the rooftops!

Home I went again, to put much right, with apologies and a real effort to be useful and part of the family. Then back to school, to pull with authority instead of against, to apologize for past wrongs, and above all to make an all-out attack against the spirit of lying, driving myself to confess every time to the one concerned, till very shame began to close my lips against the fantasies. I became a school prefect, and the head of my house. I longed to lead, and to lead well and rightly. I longed to be respected, not now for myself, exactly, but that I might lead others to put God first.

I tried earnestly to help others, to be kindly, to be sincere. I was an ardent Anglo-Catholic, regular at the confessional and the mass, every part of me stretching out after the Unseen Power who could meet all needs. And yet I was acutely conscious that He was not doing so. The needs were getting bigger; the hopelessness was more hopeless; the futility of life itself at times became almost unbearable. Whilst in church, I could lose myself to all the problems, bathed in the strange mysticism and pious ritualism; but on leaving the service, I had nothing—no power, no companion, no help to answer the daily needs and meet the daily problems.

It was this sense of emptiness and futility which led me to become a cinema fan in my holidays, to try to escape from the pointlessness of life. Every week-night and twice on Saturdays, if there were seven different films, I would try to lose myself in a make-believe world—anything to drown reality. Sometimes I would even go twice to the same film rather than suffer the boredom of an empty evening. There was a great emptiness, a great void in my life.

I helped at times at the Franciscans' headquarters in Peckham. Because of the blitz, there were no Sisters living in that area, but I loved to stay in the guest-room of the Order's Home. There was a lovely church opposite, very still and quiet, in the midst of the rush of traffic, the whine of the air-raid warnings, the sufferings and poverty of the people around. Flickering lights burned in the red crucibles in front of each altar. All else was dim, with a vague sense of the unreal. I would creep in, and upstairs to the gallery, along to the Lady Chapel, many times in a day, seeking an explanation, a companion, a comfort to my heart's loneliness. Every three hours, the Franciscan monks had prayers there, and I knelt in the shadows, and drank in of their piety. Then back I would go to the poor tenement building opposite, with its rickety stairs, uncarpeted floors, peeling paint, and its many and varied visitors—mothers in distress for sons missing in the war; mothers in dire need of coal or food or clothing; mothers in depravity, in immorality and loose living—all came, and were helped, and went away comforted. In the evenings, there was the 'Club' for young people, teenagers who had been turned away from the Civic Centre Club for one reason or another, young men and women often from most unsavoury backgrounds. The dancing, endless records, and open rottenness; the weakness, and weariness and emptiness of life—I saw it all, but took no part. I had no interest, no awakened desires, just an apathy.

And all the while, God was driving me to see that in myself there was nothing, absolutely nothing of any worth. It became at moments almost a desperate fight—the knowledge that God held the key, the answer; that He could make sense of it all; that without Him, it was a weary, stupid, empty, pointless, useless life. The burden of the world's need was crushing, overwhelming. Only God could meet it, could answer it; and yet, where was He? How could I find Him? How could I become part of His pattern, and lose myself in Him?

# 2

# Climbing to the Top

I left school a few weeks before the end of the summer term 1944, in order to have a short holiday and prepare to go to Cambridge for the 'long vac' term. This was a war emergency measure, enabling doctors to complete their nine-term university course in two years by making compulsory the fourth term from July to September each year, during the long vacation. My father met me in London and took me to a show—one of the Gilbert and Sullivan operas.

It was the time of the V1 'doodle-bugs' and everyone was tense and fearful. There was little chattering in the streets and shops. When the siren alerted us of an approaching raid, everyone hurried quickly on their own business. Then someone caught the high whine of a V1 and stood still, looking up. The action was infectious. We almost felt the very traffic stand still and draw in its breath, and all London waited. The whine grew; faces were strained. Each one knew we should make for shelters, but we had done it too often, and even shelters were not proof against these new weapons. A fascination was on us. Suddenly, there was a sharp silence— a great pause hung in the air-then an explosion, a rumble, and a gentle sigh caught up and multiplied, as each walker hurried on his way, secretly ashamed of the first thought, 'I'm safe this time.' The urgency of self-preservation amidst all the fear and uncertainty, almost pushed into second place the thought, 'Poor beggars, I wonder who got that one?'

And so I reached Newnham College, Cambridge, at the end of July, found my way to Clough Hall, and discovered from a list on the noticeboard that I had been allocated room 8a, a small room, usually the bedroom attached to the larger sitting-room. The latter was to be a bedsitter for this extra term, to enable the new 'freshers' to be accommodated. The place seemed vast and empty and silent. A cold fear of loneliness clutched at my throat. Why had I come? I felt that I would never fit into college life. I knew no-one. My trunk was pushed against the communicating door and, to try and calm my yearning to run away and leave it all, I started urgently to unstrap and unpack. Having piled everything on the small bed, and pushed books on the two small shelves over its head, I turned to place things in the drawers of the chest. I glanced at my pale sallow face in the mirror, and the untidy plaits hanging down over my shoulders—and noticed a card stuck in the frame. Leaning forward, with my arms full of clothes, I read, 'If you don't know anyone, and have nowhere to go after supper, come and have coffee in my room, no. 12, at 8 p.m.' It was signed 'Dorothy'. My eyes blurred, and a lump filled my throat. I quickly finished unpacking, my mind excited, homesick and fearful by turns.

A bell sounded, and I slipped into the corridor and watched and waited. Others walked by, chatting and nonchalant, and I joined the stream towards the 'hall'. It was still war days, and food rationing was strict, yet a good meal was served us at the serving-tables, each one collecting what they wished individually. The other students were friendly and would have drawn me into their conversation, but an overwhelming shyness (from a sense of inferiority, or a fear of not being able to hold my own) kept me a grim prisoner. Soon their conversation drifted into their own channels, and my monosyllabic replies became unnecessary. Tears pricked my eyes—my very first day, and I had raised up a barrier that I had vowed should never stand again! I wasn't hungry, yet didn't dare to leave, not knowing the rules. So I made a mockery of eating, following the lead of others.

Back in my room after supper, my loneliness and fear of this vast place with its swarms of intellectual students became so intense, the feeling of being submerged and lost in it all so real, that I lay numbly on my bed and planned how to write home and ask them to let me leave.

I must have dozed from sheer weariness of mental strain. Wasn't that a clock striking? Glancing quickly at my watch, I remembered the invitation—8 p.m. at no. 12. I ran to the bathroom, washed my face, and made my way along the corridor. Knocking at the door of no. 12, I entered, and Dorothy glanced up, her face red, smoke swirling around her, as she knelt by the hearth, trying to coax a fire into existence! 'Can you make a fire?' The straight forward, urgent appeal, the complete acceptance of a total stranger in her room, the absurdity of the smoking pile in the grate on a hot, sticky, July evening, and the barriers were gone! We soon had a kettle on a cheerful blaze, and a group of about eight of us, I think, sat around on chairs, sofa, bed and floor, chatting about everything and nothing. I never quite knew who were newcomers like myself, and who were 'old stagers'. I don't remember much of all the chatter. I believe the coffee tasted a good deal of smoke and paraffin, but I know I slept well that night, with a quiet feeling of security that I had a friend.

Next day, Dot called for me for breakfast; and later took me down town, showing me the quickest way to the Anatomy block: then on to the shopping centre, to see which shops were the cheapest, and which the most reliable for books, equipment, stationery, and so on. Home we went to lunch, then back again to sign on for afternoon lectures and to arrange about tutorials. She was with me all through that day. That was Dorothy. I am glad to say she eventually got her own degree, as well as helping crowds of us to settle in and to get ours.

The Anatomy Dissection Room! Never will I forget the first day, and my sense of unutterable horror. The very smell of formalin today brings back a wave of memories. The crowds, the noise of chatter and instruments, the growing silence through the morning as concentration mounted, the greasy books propped open on the benches to show their brightly coloured, tidy diagrams of the pale mess we were handling—and to me, always a sense of unreality, of horror, almost of foreboding. I developed a deep sense of revulsion that almost paralyzed my thinking capacity. A demonstrator coming round, neatly sorting out one strand from the higgledy-piggledy mass in front of me, and demanding name, description, origin, was one of the daily nightmares of the next three years that began to crush my hopes.

A paralysis seemed to settle over my mind each day at 9 a.m. as I entered the lecture theatre. All I had studied the night before seemed wiped out, like a clean slate. The lecturer's words never penetrated, owing to the gnawing fear that he might ask me a question and reveal my ignorance to all. And by 5 p.m., as I stumbled out of the block, and found my bicycle, joining the stream of humanity, I felt bowed and unable to face any more study. Fortunately, that first term, there were no tutorials, or I really might have given up and gone home!

Then came the first Saturday. What a wonderful sense of freedom! I lay in bed late in the morning, and wandered to the notice-boards after breakfast. Pinned up was a list for any to sign who would like to play cricket in the afternoon. Dare I? I loved it, but I hadn't been any good at school—and here they were probably all excellent. 'Hallo,' said a voice behind me. 'Do you play?' and there was a tall broad girl, with a beaming smile and thick wavy hair. 'I'd like to try', I replied diffidently. And that was the beginning of another friendship—with the cricket captain for the coming year. I was assured somewhat jokingly that if I knew which end of the bat to hold I'd be in the team! We had a wonderful afternoon, about fourteen of us. I wasn't good, by any stretch of imagination, but I was far from being the worst!

After tea, we went on the river in a punt. I was thrilled not only by the actual novelty of the experience and the loveliness of the countryside from Cambridge to Grantchester, but above all by the natural friendliness of the other girls, the very fact that they appeared to want me to join them. We went bathing together in the Grantchester pool. It was all wonderful and new, and I determinedly set about forgetting the past misgivings and fears, my insecurity and need.

On Sunday, I got up early and went down town to Little St Mary to early mass. The quiet reverence, the sense of mystery, the peace was all as I knew it, and yet no-one spoke to me as I entered or as I left. I went again at eleven and saw several students there, but again there was no gesture of friendliness or welcome—and none of my little group of new friends was there. The day dragged on, but without the usual happiness of a Sunday. In the evening, I went to St Benedict's Church, where the Franciscans worshipped. I spoke to one at the close of the service, mentioning my friendship with Father Charles. He was courteous, but distant—certainly not welcoming, nor proffering any invitation of friendship. I felt hurt and puzzled as I cycled home, and went to bed supperless since I had missed 'hall'. I didn't see any of my new friends about and realized anew the old pangs of loneliness.

And so a pattern began to set in, and with it a sense of belonging, and thus security; a pattern of work, and study, mingled with friendships and Saturday outings. On certain days, however, Dorothy and the others didn't join us after hall. When I asked about this one week, she told me they had a prayer-meeting daily between early and late hall, and a Bible study together, once a week after halls. Would I care to go? Certainly! And so I went to my first Bible study and sat amazed as someone unfolded the mysteries of Ephesians 3, and even more amazed as they discussed it afterwards and freely quoted other parts of Scripture to support their arguments. Going back to our rooms later on, after a cup of cocoa and biscuits, I shared with Dot my amazement at their knowledge of the Bible and understanding of its contents. With a kindly smile, she suggested that I should go regularly.

The following Sunday we met at late hall, and she asked what I was doing afterwards. Would I care to go with her to a Christian address? I had cut evening service and was feeling a little guilty at having been caught out, but she made no comment (doubtless having been praying that she might meet me there). And so together we went to the sermon arranged by the Cambridge Inter-Collegiate Christian Union (CICCU), a regular Sunday evening activity during

University terms. We left our bicycles in the small courtyard outside and they were stolen during the service, which rather effaced any memory I might have had of the sermon's subject-matter!

And so my first term passed. I was still closely bound to the Anglo-Catholics, sensing a need of the protection of organized religion and imposed discipline to control the hungry urges of spirit and soul, and possibly also to carry the ultimate responsibility for solutions for the world's great needs without involving me. I went regularly to confessional and mass, found peace of mind in formal obedience, but lacked any friendship or encouragement there. Alongside this, were the happy, free friendships with Dorothy, Sylvia and other members of the Christian Union—games and outings together, sitting together for meals and, later, for the Bible studies and Sunday evening services—friendships that were open and clean and healthy. Their lives and faces radiated a happiness and peace that was very nearly infectious, and quite obviously satisfying. It was thrilling, just tasting the wonder of this level of friendship and of communion. Yet some inner fear, or reserve, kept me back from definitely identifying myself with them, so that I always remained just a little apart.

Four weeks' holiday followed, back with the family in our new home in south-east London—a lovely big house and a marvellous garden. And yet I missed my new friends and longed for the next term to start. My school-girl sisters all seemed very young and immature. And I don't doubt that to them I seemed stand-offish and a prig! The first 'V2s' fell at this stage, and there were sufferings and shortages on all sides. The parish church had been badly bombed and we now met in a hall behind the Methodist church. But I did not appreciate the way the Vicar took the service, and missed so much the elaborate ritualism to which I was accustomed that I was not over-bothered about going regularly.

My second term began with mixed feelings, joy in renewed friendship and dread of the growing pressure of work, augmented by the fear of tutorials. Slowly, I began to slip into the habit of joining the CU for the prayer meetings as well as for Bible studies. Then on Sundays, I began going to church with them, sometimes Congregational, sometimes Brethren, sometimes Evangelical Church of England. Mr Kenneth Hooker, I remember, preached the Freshers' Sermon on 1 Timothy 2:5-6. I was stirred and challenged. I learned new hymns and choruses, and enjoyed the bright, alert singing. Even now I can remember the first time I sang, 'More about Jesus would I know....' My whole being was deeply stirred. We were sitting round the fire in Sylvia's room for a Bible study one evening, late in October. I don't remember the study—the words of the hymn kept repeating in my mind. When the others dispersed, I stayed sitting on the rug, gazing into the fire, with a great longing stirring in my innermost soul. 'More about Jesus would I know....' As we sat, the two of us, in complete, unbroken stillness, it was as though a window opened and slowly, amazedly, in stunned awe, I glimpsed through—a twig sputtered on the fire, and it was lost. Again, urgently, holding on to the moment, willing the very presence of Jesus to become real to my soul, the glory seemed to shine, a light of great brightness. I hardly dared to breathe; it felt as though life was suspended, caught up, breathless. My heart filled with joy and wonder—and it passed. With a sigh, I turned to Sylvia. She was praying. It was already the early hours of a new day. We did not talk; I slipped away to my room.

During that Christmas term, I think I reached a mental assent that the presentation of the gospel offered by the CU members was true, though I remained unconvinced that this need clash with ritualistic practice in church worship. I was tremendously intrigued by their love of Scripture, and I began to read avidly. I started at Matthew and slogged through to the end of the New Testament that term. Slowly, I became gripped by it. First I read with them, then I read on my own, with a growing hunger to know what it was all about and to know the One who had written it. Everything began to fit into a pattern. I could see that they had something that I did not, and a great desire to have it myself was born. I stopped going to other meetings and other churches. I went to all the CU activities I could—Bible studies, prayer meetings, missionary study groups, open-airs, church meetings. I agreed to it all in my mind. And the joy of new friends, the great happiness of being an accepted one of this new crowd, made life seem very good. As far as they were concerned, they believed I was truly 'converted', and told me so. But as yet I had no peace, no heart satisfaction. The sense of need was still there, with the niggling question, 'Are you sure this is real?' I was sure it was real and the truth; but I was also conscious that I lacked something.

Then two other demands entered into fierce competition. One of the SPG home workers came on a visit to Cambridge for a long weekend in late November and especially asked to see me. I did not want to meet her; I did not want to face again the conflicting loyalties. But I could not politely refuse. The evening's talk left me unsettled, unhappy, yet completely unconvinced. Her argument about the sacraments, the mass and the confessional in particular, no longer rang with authority as in the past. Her plea seemed to rest only on the historical symbolism of the church and not on scriptural reality. She stressed that in the church, symbolized by the priest, was stored all truth and the only means of salvation. The accent was on works, regular attendance at church, full confession, implicit obedience to all church discipline, and the receiving of grace only by the divinely appointed means of the sacraments in the hands of the priest. There was so much I did not understand. I felt so weak and helpless, like a baby, unable to answer her, or to give a reasoned explanation of my newly awakening faith. Why did I no longer need the doctrine of consubstantiation, the real presence of Christ in the elements at the mass? How dared I ignore the church's recognized means of grace? I did not know the answer then. All I had was an indefinable realization that something was missing, something wrong. 1 Timothy 2:5-6, the text of the Freshers' Sermon, came back vividly. 'There is…one mediator between God and men, the man Christ Jesus.' Nowhere in the New Testament had I read of the priesthood being invested in a human priest who could act as a go-between between myself and God.

The following weekend Father Charles came, and I loved him, simply and sincerely. I went to confessional on the Saturday evening, and to services all day Sunday where he was ministering and preaching. Again the old mystical attraction drew me and enfolded me, and my newly awakening soul cried out for fear of being submerged once more.

The other interest which competed for my support at this time was Communism. One Saturday, that same term, I was asked to 'help out' by playing goal-keeper for the Newnham hockey team—and my luck was in! Having practically no previous interest in hockey, I became goal-keeper overnight for the Cambridge University Women's team! Here I met the captain for the year, the quiet, efficient, outspoken leader of the Cambridge University Women's Communist Party! Our rapidly flourishing friendship involved many party meetings, and the learning of the fundamentals of dialectical materialism, and of the ideology that they said could answer all the crying needs of our poverty-stricken and suffering world.

Sundays became a three-cornered battle: Anglo-Catholicism in the mornings; Communism in the afternoons; Evangelicalism in the evenings. The CU made no criticism, neither did they retract the offered friendship. They did not argue, nor seek to persuade; they just went further out of their way to draw me out and help me.

As Christmas approached, news came from home that one of my younger sisters had mumps. We had all had chickenpox together several years before and I had been very ill with it. Later we all had measles and my eyesight was permanently damaged. So it was felt best that I should avoid the mumps if possible, and therefore not go home till January. Where then for Christmas? Two kindly Methodist friends, Jean and Mary, each invited me for a week to their homes, and I had a lovely holiday with each, in keen Methodist families. But there were ten more days before the quarantine would be ended.

Dorothy and Sylvia arranged for me to go to a houseparty. They even filled in the forms, looked up the trains, and handed me the timetable of events! So on December 27th

I arrived at Mount Hermon Bible College, Ealing, with a suitcase and my fears, to join what turned out to be a gathering of keen Christian women training as officers for young people's camps and houseparties for the coming Easter and summer. I was like a duck out of water! I shared a dormitory with other girls of my own age—including a bright, red-headed girl of nineteen next to me, whose brother was a medical student in my year at Cambridge. I remember they all seemed to have plenty of money, and I had practically none! Afternoons were free, and they all went sightseeing, or to the ice-rink-and I stayed at home, ostensibly to study, unwilling to let them know that I could not afford it! It was cold—the last winter of the war, and coal rationing was severe. We huddled eiderdowns over our knees as we sat in the study room for morning Bible study and discussion groups. I bought a lovely new Bible complete with a commentary.

On the second day, we were led in a study through the book of Genesis, shown how to summarize it, get hold of it, divide it up, and then share it with others. I was fascinated and took detailed notes. My ignorance of Scripture was appalling. Our leader told us that the day after tomorrow we would do the same with the book of Romans and suggested that we each try to read through it beforehand. I bought the IVF Search the Scriptures (a Bible study course prepared to help students). The next evening, after supper, I curled up by the fire in the sitting-room, and started out into Romans. I read. I studied each suggested question. I wrote the answer in the margin of my lovely new Bible. Time ticked on. I reached the end. With a satisfied sigh, I closed my Bible, uncurled my stiff and cold legs, and slipped quietly upstairs to bed. On the landing, I met two girls coming from the bathroom. 'You're late', I said. 'You're early', they rejoined with a grin. I slipped into my bedroom, to find that it was 6.30 a.m. and these girls were getting up for kitchen duty! Later that morning, in Bible study, I fell asleep and missed the very session for which I had spent all night preparing! But Romans has remained one of my 'favourite' books of Scripture ever since. Through its orderly array of facts, its clear systematic presentation of doctrine, I gripped the essential basic truth of man's need in his lost state of sin and depravity, and of God's provision to meet that need through the substitutionary death of Christ, of His wonderful power to make this provision real and vital to each individual by the work of the Holy Spirit, and, even more, of His amazing desire for fellowship and communion with us, His adopted children, by the daily indwelling and outworking of His same Spirit.

I sat through meeting after meeting and filled an exercise book with notes. I talked things over with many of the staff. I heard the different doctrines being carefully and accurately expounded, supported by Scripture. My mind could grasp it, and begin to take in the tremendousness of its import. I was beginning to get the 'jargon', yet I knew in my heart that I hadn't got Him.

The last evening of the houseparty there had been a bit of a row at the supper table and some sharp disagreements, largely revolving around denominational practices, particularly differing ways of celebrating the Holy Communion service. I had spoken up, albeit diffidently, in defence of the doctrine of consubstantiation, the 'real' presence of Christ in the elements of bread and wine. Had not Jesus said, 'This is my body...this is my blood'? But I became heated when laughed at. They asked if I could be truly converted if I was such a Romanist at heart?

I left the room and rushed upstairs, bitterly ashamed of having been drawn into the argument and losing control of myself. I gazed out of the window, and heard the happy chattering of the others down below. My mind went back through that week and all its teachings, through the past term and the multitudes of new influences and new friendships, back to my home and family and childhood. Suddenly, I flung myself on my bed, in a flood of tears and loneliness. With an overwhelming sense of failure and helplessness, I cried out to God (if there was a God) to meet with me and to make utterly real and vital to me Himself. I raised my eyes, and through my tears read a text on the wall: 'Be still, and know that I am God' (Ps. 46:10). That was all. Immediately the whole burden fell away in a moment. Be still and know God, whose name is 'I am'. Be still and know Him. Stop going to this one and that; stop striving to understand with the intellect. Just be still, and know Him. In that moment, a great flood of peace and joy and unutterable happiness flooded in, and I knew that He and I had entered into a new relationship. I knew God, and I knew in that moment that all the theories were true, and somehow He would work them out for me. The steady reading of Scripture in the previous months, the careful listening to doctrinal teaching both at the houseparty and in Christian Union meetings, had prepared the way. For years the Holy Spirit had been opening my eyes to a sense of sin, convicting me of my unworthiness before a Holy God. But now came the wonderful gift of repentance. God poured out His grace in forgiveness, in cleansing from all the uncleanness of sin, and in revealing, at this time, the amazing wonder of the friendship of Christ.

I went downstairs walking on air. Some of the other campers said afterwards, 'Your face was absolutely shining and we knew something had happened.' I went into the sitting-room and joined the rest for the final meeting. We sang a few choruses (I remember that I didn't know any of them!) and then our leader opened the meeting for testimonies. I didn't know what she meant by a 'testimony', so I waited. Silence reigned! She made another attempt to get us talking by pointing out what a blessing it could be to testify to others. Still dead silence! 'Well, hasn't anyone anything to tell of what God has done for her during the week?' I understood that and opened my mouth—and suddenly found I'd nothing to say! I who had been accustomed to speaking at any time, on any subject, found I was tongue-tied with an intense helplessness. I just didn't know what to say. I knew something had happened, and as I sat there with my mouth open, I eventually somehow blurted out that I had met with God, and He had forgiven me and...that was all! Dr Graham Scroggie, a veteran Christian and much-loved Bible teacher, was there. He wrote in my new Bible Philippians 3:10, 'That I may know him, and the power of his resurrection, and the fellowship of his sufferings, being made conformable unto his death.' He said to me, 'Tonight you've entered into the first part of the verse, "That I may know him." This is only the beginning, and there's a long journey ahead. My prayer for you is that you will go on through the verse to know "the power of his resurrection" and also, God willing, one day perhaps, "the fellowship of his sufferings, being made conformable unto his death." And so started for me the thrilling journey of the Christian pilgrimage through this earthly life towards the heavenly eternity.

# 3

# Enjoying the View

I went home the next day wearing a bright new Scripture Union badge and carrying a shiny new Bible. In the crowded compartment of the slow Victoria–Bromley train a man diagonally across the carriage from me asked what my badge stood for. A little embarrassed, I explained that members of the Scripture Union undertook to read a set passage from the Bible each day, believing that it was God's book and that it would help them to live good lives. He asked for further explanations. Raising my voice against the noise of the engine and the wheels, I sought to reply, very conscious of the curious, rather antagonistic, looks of the other ten passengers, disturbed in their happy solitude. Red in the face, but determined not to run from the challenge, I told him of my conversion the day before, and of the battle that led up to it, including my real longing to know God and to obey Him. Our conversation continued until Shortlands where, with a sigh of relief, I stumbled out, only to find myself followed by my questioner! Quietly, he placed a hand on my shoulder and wished me God's richest blessing in my new life. The surprised look on my face made him smile. Then he explained that my brand-new badge and Bible had told their own story and he had deliberately drawn me out to testify in public to help me start out in the way I should go on! I later found that he was a keen member of Christ Church, Bromley, which fellowship I myself soon joined.

Now began a period of great joy. Everything was wonderful. I loved every moment, every meeting, every opportunity for testimony. I had the inestimable joy of knowing that Christ was my Saviour. I joined the Cambridge Women's Inter-Collegiate Christian Union, and enjoyed fellowship with many new friends. I revelled in the security of being publicly committed. I had, as it were, burned my boats. I gave up going to the cinema and lost my desire to join in many of the activities which were merely the done thing—drink, smoking, make-up and dancing— none of which had ever held any very real attraction for me personally. I wrote to my father and to the board of directors of my school who were paying my college fees, to tell them that I was now studying medicine to be a missionary. In all honesty, I felt I must let them know just in case it affected their desire to continue paying for my education. Both wrote back and assured me that they were delighted and would continue to support me.

To be a missionary? I had known for years that I was going to be a missionary. Would my conversion change this? Did I need some further specific call? I had already, however, signified my intention of serving God abroad by joining the Inter-Varsity Missionary Fellowship, and the urge in my heart towards overseas missionary service was growing greater, not diminishing. It began to seem to me the obvious Christian duty of one and all. I was puzzled by others' lack of interest in missionary service, their lack of concern for the millions who were in darkness, who had never heard of the love of God.

Bible study was an excitement in those early days. I remember being fascinated by a series of ten Bible readings on the Song of Solomon. Next term we were going to study Hebrews 11 for ourselves, and Sylvia, our Christian Union leader, said that I was to lead the third study on verse 3: 'Through faith we understand that the worlds were framed by the word of God...' I spent hours with her preparing that study, and I learnt more perhaps in its preparation than in all I heard others teach in the following weeks. It set for me the pattern for the future, of thorough, accurate Bible searching and digging. It impressed me with my appalling ignorance of Scripture. All I had was a vague rudimentary knowledge of some well-known children's stories, but with no real idea of where they came, nor of their context. Sylvia was studying Psalm 119 in the early mornings of each day and had made a beautiful and exquisitely neat chart of it, on one huge sheet, in all its sections. On this chart she was underlining in different colours each line of thought throughout the Psalm, and one could see a pattern emerging. To watch her studying the Bible in this way, to see her obvious love of it, stirred up in me a great desire to know more. Since my conversion, I had also started Dr Graham Scroggie's four-year Bible Correspondence Course, which meant, roughly speaking, studying a book a month. From 7–8 each morning was one of the happiest hours of the day, reading, studying, underlining, comparing, learning Scripture. And slowly it was taking possession, the new affection replacing the old.

Then there was a growing realization of the possibilities of prayer. In April 1945, I went to the IVF Student Conference in Oxford. Again, the old shyness of meeting new faces and the fear of being asked things I did not know, tended to shut me up within myself. Everything was a bit high-powered. Open discussion groups tended to depress me as everybody else seemed to know much more than I did! But the prayer sessions were the great moments of each day. God drew near in those seasons of prayer, and I began to learn the liberty of the outpoured heart. Mildred Mitchell, daughter of the Home Director of the China Inland Mission, was there, and was a great help to me. She and I, and another friend with whom I was sharing a room, had a discussion late into the night about guidance. How, we asked, can one be sure of knowing God's will? I remember her summarizing on her fingers in the following order:

1. Daily Bible reading, when He can speak to us through a passage, an example or a warning;
2. Daily private prayer, when we talk the problem over with the Lord; as we wait on Him in quietness, He can speak directly to our hearts;

3. The advice of Christian friends and those of greater experience, who may have had to make a similar decision in the past;

4. One's circumstances, including family or business commitments, health or even finance.

Then she moved her thumb to and fro in front of her fingers and said, 'Peace—in each one, in turn, individually and together. Let the peace of God umpire in your heart; if He is speaking He will give peace and silence other voices.' I still use the same basic principles in guidance today.

Then came the problem of sport. I had played in goal for the hockey team that season, and now the cricket season was starting. I loved the exercise, and perhaps again I was influenced by the feeling that I could achieve something, gain my blue, prove to myself that I wasn't useless! But it all took time—daily practices down at the nets, and games or matches every Saturday. So I, and other Christians involved, began to pray about it and God challenged us to use our sport as a medium of evangelism, and to seek the captain of the team for Himself. That summer our cricket captain was a Christian Scientist. She and I were great friends and enjoyed being together. As a result, I began going to many meetings with her to learn what she believed and, in exchange, she came to a few of ours. Slowly, the warmth of friendship offered in the Christian Union, and the obvious sincerity and warmth of conviction, backed up so solidly with scriptural accuracy, began to win her towards our faith. But in particular, she was influenced by our growing friendship and intimacy. For me, it was a wonderful day in the summer of 1945 when she openly declared herself for Christ and broke away from the Christian Scientists. I believed she was my first 'convert', and it was with a deep sense of grief that I came to realize a few years later that she was won by my persuasiveness and personality, rather than by the beauty and power of Christ. The former could not hold her, nor establish her, nor satisfy her, except along a fleshly level of human friendship. Only the latter could have given her new life, and strength and joy and courage. Many times since I have had to be careful not to over-persuade folk, nor to draw them only by the strength of my own rather dominant personality.

In the summer of 1945 I went to my first camp as a junior medical officer. What an exciting, wonderful fortnight! There were some six Christian women as Camp Officers, and fifty or so junior teenage girls. We had hired a lovely boarding school at Chumleigh, Devon, to give the girls a first-rate country holiday for a fortnight. I remember so clearly VJ Day which celebrated the defeat of Japan and the end of those six long years of war. One of my jobs at camp was seeing to the cleanliness of the toilets—and we had a mild epidemic of summer diarrhoea! At the 8 a.m. staff meeting, I mentioned our urgent need of toilet paper to our Commandant so that she could add it to her shopping list. Just then the telephone rang. It was the local Vicar giving us the news of Japan's surrender and warmly inviting us all to a united service of thanksgiving in the village. 'Oh', I exclaimed in horror, 'the shops will all be shut. Whatever shall we do for toilet paper?' The group got down to praise and prayer for all the events of the day and the spiritual wellbeing of each young camper. Then the Commandant, in her closing prayer, reminded the Lord of our need of toilet paper. I think I was shocked! Certainly I was amazed that one could dare bring such a topic to the Almighty!

Later in the morning, we all walked down to the church and attended the united thanksgiving. As we left afterwards, one pleasant faced man came up to me, and said how very pleased they all were to welcome us to their village and to their fellowship, adding with a smile that he was the local grocer and would be delighted to do anything he could to help us. I blurted out my tale of woe, our need of toilet paper! And in half an hour, twelve rolls were delivered to the school where we were staying. Truly God had answered prayer.

Near the end of camp, we had an 'object-service'. The youngsters all went out, two by two, to collect or make some object mentioned in the Bible. These objects were all gathered on the table in the meeting-room, each with a small label giving the Scripture reference of where this object could be found. There was a piece of bread: 'I am the bread of life'; a wild flower: 'even Solomon in all his glory was not arrayed like one of these'; a bunch of grapes referring to those brought back by the twelve spies of Moses' time; a jawbone calling to mind one of Samson's exploits. There were many others, among them a lovely plaited ring of thorns. The text attached to this was Mark 15:17, 'And they... platted a crown of thorns, and put it about his head.' At prayers that evening each leader in turn spoke a few words on one of the objects. I was terribly nervous. I had never tried to speak before without hours of careful preparation! I gazed at the table in a sort of numb horror, and the crown of thorns stood out so clearly, I could not see anything else. I was number four to speak—and I willed the others not to choose the crown of thorns! Eventually I stood up to take my turn, lifted up the carefully plaited ring, and then closed my eyes in a sudden wave of nausea from sheer panic. My heart was pounding; my mouth felt dry. Somehow I pulled myself together, and spoke of His suffering in my place, His receiving my condemnation. At last it was all over. One of the staff mentioned afterwards how touched she had been to see my earnest prayer before I spoke—and my heart lurched! Yet in the years ahead, I was to learn that she had been more accurate than I then dared to believe, as I discovered new avenues of prayer, when, as Paul puts it in Romans 8, the Spirit groans within us and our hearts go out to God in wordless prayer as we do battle with the unseen powers of darkness, knowing nothing but a horror and fear of failure.

During the next Christmas term life continued to be very full and wonderful and worth while. I was asked to become an executive member of the Christian Union for the coming year. When reading the doctrinal basis which I would need to sign, I was struck by the statement that I believed the whole Bible to be the inspired word of God. I had not yet read it all, and felt I could not honestly sign this until I had read it right through. This stiffened me to a concentrated effort to complete my first reading of the Old Testament by Christmas, before the end of my first exciting year as a newly born-again Christian. I was deeply stirred at the thought of being trusted with leadership. I had always longed to lead, and now strangely I feared it. I felt so unable, yet knew that I could rely on His enabling.

During the term I was asked to go to the home of Dr Joyce Goodchild at Nottingham to give my testimony at an informal Saturday evening meeting. This was another milestone; my first public speaking engagement! I remember preparing with such infinite care and practising in the bath, speaking to the taps, timing myself exactly to the limits I had been given. What a thrilling and wonderful weekend that was! Every new experience seemed to be just one more part of this new mountain-top of joy, one more view over the glorious surrounding peaks. It was to be the start of a precious friendship, and forerunner of several such meetings in the coming year.

I was chosen to play goalkeeper not only for the University Women's team, but also for Cambridge County Ladies hockey team, along with Olga, the University captain, and Jessie, another Newnham undergraduate. Together we set out for Colchester in the week after Christmas for the week's tournament of Eastern Counties at Clacton. We lived at the Girls' Friendly Society Hostel at Colchester, sharing together an attic dormitory, since Clacton was out of reach of our student allowances! The first night there, I fought, as many others have done, the brief battle with pride and self-consciousness, and then got down on my knees by my bedside for prayer. They were both quiet till I climbed into bed. Then in the dark, Olga (the leader of the University Women's Communist Party!) bluntly demanded the point of what I had done. What benefit did I think prayer was? I knew so little how to explain, but I tried to share my assurance of the truths I had learned during the past year. Throughout the week, at meals, on buses, in the evening round the sitting-room fire, we argued Communism versus Christianity. I felt very helpless and seemed to make no impact on Olga at all. Jessie just listened and watched, but during next term she quietly joined the Christian Union. She was never very dramatic, just quietly sure of Christ's love for her and her love for Him. What a joy and encouragement this was to me, even as I saw Olga slipping away from us and apparently hardening against us.

In July I went to Keswick with Dr Goodchild. We were to be a mixed bunch, about eighteen of us, in three big bell-tents. Three were girls from Nottingham University, Mary and myself from Newnham, and the rest were factory and shop girls, many of whom had been converted during the previous year at Dr Goodchild's Saturday night At Homes. It was a memorable Keswick for me. Dr Goodchild, Mary and I went a day earlier than the rest to set up camp. First we had to scythe the long grass! It was blisteringly hot, the end of a heatwave, and it was exciting pitching the tents and preparing. Food rationing was still severe. That week, bread, cakes and flour rationing commenced. We managed to procure all necessary permits and bought the week's stores—a tongue, the week's butter ration, etc. These were placed in large basins in the small stream at the bottom of the field. We went to the station to meet the other campers and returned to find the butter gone, basin and all! We reported our grievous loss to the police, and set about helping everyone to unpack, to make palliasses and to settle in. I felt sure the thief would return for the tongue! As dark fell, I slipped from our tent and sat on the running board of the car, facing a hole in the hedge the other side of the stream, with a large mallet on my knees—my one urgent prayer that the Lord would not let me kill him! I heard him approach; I raised the mallet; he neared the hole; I sneezed! And he fled!

The camp presented great difficulties. Despite sincere efforts on the part of the student element to prevent it, we found ourselves divided into two groups, university and others. Friendliness was interpreted as patronage; squabbling and petty unkindnesses started and it looked as though the whole purpose of the camp would be wrecked. Then the rain came—and it poured steadily for three days! The field was a quagmire, the stream a rushing torrent; everything was soaking and there was no way of drying it. Then I became ill. Frantically, Dr Goodchild sought for a solution. The Convention secretary came to our aid, and arranged for us to have the loan of the local drill-hall. The IVF men came over and cleaned it out for us, loaned us camp beds and dry blankets, and started a shuttle service to move us in. Now we were all together in one big room around a central table, except for Dr Goodchild in a little side room. And I lay ill on her bed with a mild attack of pneumonia. When everyone was settled in, she joined them for a short prayer meeting. Together they praised God for everyone's kindness to us and His provision for us, and prayed for His outpoured blessing and especially for my speedy recovery. Immediately, He began to work. Apologies were made, new friendships began as they all mixed together. I recovered quickly. We were all deeply conscious of the Lord being vitally in our midst.

There followed in the summer another, and longer, camp at Weston-super-Mare, to which secondary schoolgirls from all over England came. Again it was far from easy. To begin with there were divisions among the leaders, some of them denominational in their origin, others arising from differences in their approach to the whole question of discipline. The campers were quick to sense the lack of unity among the officers. Rules were broken continuously and at one stage near-anarchy reigned! Instead of the usual harmless ragging and fun we were faced with vicious and spiteful gang warfare. During that camp, however, I began to sense clearly His hand upon me for leadership. There was a new sense of dignity, a great assurance of His will, a fresh vision of what I believed He yearned to do for us and through us. I was conscious that the girls responded to me and appeared to respect me, and this gave me a deeper desire to help them. I was not myself deeply involved in the staff difficulties, since I was a relative outsider. This gave me more time to be quiet and on my own. It was at these times that different girls came to me with their problems, and I was amazed to see how the Lord gave me the words to help them. Then I found a great longing to take a series of Bible studies with any who wanted to come, and I readily obtained permission for this from the other staff. In those meetings I 'found my feet' and began to realize that He was giving me a gift of imparting to others that which was precious to me.

The following Christmas term, at the start of my third year, a member of the CU executive and with a great desire to win other students for Christ, I faced up to His demand for complete, unquestioning obedience. I felt that this involved me in Believer's Baptism as a public testimony to my faith. Asking the advice of certain spiritual leaders at Cambridge, I was shaken by their apparent antagonism, one of them even quoting Galatians 3:1-3 to me. I became convinced in my own mind, however, that my spiritual advancement towards maturity in Christ demanded this step of obedience, even though it might lose me Christian friends and valued fellowship. Possibly this was for me the first touch, the first hint, of the years of loneliness that lay ahead, though I knew nothing of this then. I went to Nottingham to stay with Dr Goodchild for a weekend in November, and I was baptized at her church. It did not mean anything definite so far as a new experience in grace was concerned, but for me it was a definite step of obedience.

Every third year the Christian Union in Cambridge organized a Mission to the whole university. The time for this was now upon us. We had been preparing for weeks. Every day had meetings arranged. We had given out leaflets and personal invitations and it was easily our greatest concerted effort of evangelism of my three years at the university. On the Saturday previously, Olga had arrived at my room to borrow my hockey tackle (I wasn't playing that year because of the Mission, and also because of my tripos!). In the evening she returned and I offered her a bath—a luxury to her as she now lived in very poor digs as a research student in nuclear physics. She accepted gratefully after a little pressure. Because of the shortage of coal, baths were still rationed. She then joined me round the fire for hot buttered crumpets! We had been praying hard; it was a long time since we had had any contact with her. She was friendly and open, obviously lonely, and enjoying being with us. We invited her to the Mission and she agreed to come.

An amazing week followed. I seemed to live for Olga's conversion. I was round at her digs all hours. I waited for her for meetings. We discussed and argued, I prayed and wept.

For the first time since I entered Newnham, I incurred late gate fines, and Miss Chrystal, my hall tutor, was so thrilled to think I was coming out of my shell, she paid them for me! And on the last day of the Mission Olga acknowledged a mental assent to the truth of the gospel. Then a fight began. We read and studied, prayed and discussed together till all hours. I obtained leave to stay up in Cambridge for the first week of our vacation to stay with her in her digs. I yearned over her in a way I had never previously experienced. At last she said that unless God Himself revealed to her heart the assurance of her salvation, she would not go on believing. Doubts poured into my soul; I nearly lost my own faith. Could God fail her? Was it possibly not true? To me, this was just a glimpse of the great agony of identification to which we are called. I held on, almost in blind faith, almost in despair. And just before Christmas, peace came. Olga quietly knew a tremendous assurance and depth of reality. She was hungry for fellowship, Bible study, knowledge, everything she could receive. In January we went together to Nottingham and she, too, was baptized.

A few weeks later, at the beginning of the Lent term, Princess Aida Desta of Ethiopia came into my room and said that she had just received a letter from the Headmistress of Clarendon, her old school, telling of their urgent need of a matron as their own had suddenly taken ill. We got down on our knees and laid this need before the Lord. As we arose there was a knock at the door. Olga came in and blurted out: 'I've given up my job; it seems inconsistent with my faith as a Christian. Pray for me that God will show me what he wants me to do now.' Within ten minutes we were on the phone to Clarendon to ask if Olga would be suitable as assistant matron. That weekend she went to take up her new duties! It was there that she assisted at the annual China Inland Mission Conference and received her clear call to missionary service; and for many years now she and her husband, Douglas Abrahams, have been preaching and teaching the gospel in Japan.

In March, I had two amazing dreams on consecutive nights, all the more extraordinary as I very rarely dream.

The first was a walk alone across snow-covered fields, very white and dazzling. There was a road up the hill, with a fork, leading down through dark sombre pines. Suddenly a garish farm-wagon, in gaudy red and green, came roaring down the hill, skidded, slewed down into the pine forest, and was soon lost to view. Then the deep impenetrable silence fell again. I drew my eyes away from watching the empty track where the lurching wagon had passed, and turning, climbed the stile and started across the white waste, climbing, climbing. My breath hurt, the cold was cruel, the pure white burned my eyes, the lonely silence weighted the frosty air. I neared the top, strangely fearful, suddenly conscious of a great destiny. Each step ached; each gasping breath tore at my chest. There was a sense of foreboding, of death. To reach the top was essential, yet it spelt death. Then came the final struggle—tremendous brightness, clarity, purity, far distant views. I felt caught away from myself, apart, separate, and I seemed to die, shrivelled in the icy cold, yet reaching out into the blazing light. I woke in a sweat of fear, and yet a sense of tremendous triumph, as though I had been vouchsafed a glimpse into the future. I reached for my Bible, opened at my daily reading, and Obadiah 17 shone out with joy, 'Upon mount Zion shall be deliverance, and there shall be holiness; and the house of Jacob shall possess their possessions.' It was a call to an utter dedication, a going forward to possess my possessions in Him, my Deliverer, my Sanctifier.

The next night again I was caught up, as it were, in a dream of great vividness and horror. It was a dream of big crowds and pressures and fear. I found myself in the streets of London, being hunted, driven, threatened by evil men, surrounded and impeded by endless traffic. All was noise and bustle and colours, confused and terrifying. Again I woke in fear, in horror, pleading Him to deliver me. And clearly a voice seemed to ring in my ears, 'They need Him!', and my life's task was unmistakably clear. He was calling me to seek and to save the lost, to be identified with them as He was, in all that wretchedness and humanity, to snatch some from the burning, the fear, the hysteria, and draw them into His peace and grace.

Finals came and went. The last weeks were a frantic rush of study, continuing late into each night. I remember as we entered our Biochemistry practicals, my best subject, the one on which I was relying to pull me up to 2nd class honours—a slip of paper was passed to me. My brother Bob, it said, who was a student at St John's College, was very ill with angina. Everything went from my thoughts. The invigilator, Dr Baldwin, came round to see our prepared notes as to what we intended to do to work out the problem set, in order to give each one permission to use the delicate apparatus, but my paper was blank. He looked at me astonished, knowing my keenness for the subject. I silently passed him the scrap of paper. Immediately seeking permission from the other examiners, he hurried me out, got me into his car, and drove off to the hospital named on the slip. There we learnt that Bob had a mild attack of Vincent's angina and would like a bottle of lemonade! With my heart at rest, we flew back to the labs and I was given the full three hours from then, and managed to pull off the desired 2nd class honours degree!

July found me travelling once again to Keswick, just two of us, on bicycles with tents, to camp under Speaker's Rock. It was a wonderful week. On the Tuesday I went up to the mountains alone and spent all night before the Lord—Miss Ruth Paxson had spoken to a women's meeting on 'That great big capital "I"' and my heart yearned to know full surrender, that it might truly be 'Not I, but Christ'; that I might fully enter into the experience and understanding of the crucified life, identified with my Saviour. Once again, I became ill at Keswick with a sort of gastric 'flu. After two days in bed, others kindly made it possible for me to go home by train instead of bicycle.

Camp followed, an exciting and enjoyable fortnight. But just at the close, the sickness caught up with me again. I managed to get home, and arrived on the day my family had left to go abroad for five weeks' holiday. I was to look after the place in their absence! For two weeks I was really ill. The doctor wanted to move me to hospital and to send for my parents, but I dissuaded him, not wishing to spoil their holiday. He then told me that I had poliomyelitis. Slowly the pains and stiffness wore off and I got better. But a great spiritual battle began to rage. During the illness, I found I didn't want to die; and now that I was getting better, I didn't want to be a missionary! This shook my faith—my faith in myself, perhaps; my faith in my experience of salvation and, since it followed so hard on the time spent at Keswick, my faith in the validity of my consecration. Yes, He began to shake everything that was shakeable, to get me free for Himself. But I wasn't sure any longer what I wanted, nor where to turn.

# 4

# Down into the Valley

Slowly, painfully, there had been growing within me during this past year a sense of incompleteness, a gnawing fear that possibly I wasn't being absolutely honest. Outwardly everything was fine! I was a leader of the Christian Union, a keen promoter of missionary interest, an ardent student of the Bible, as well as being a third-year undergraduate with hockey and cricket blues. Yet there was a feeling of cloaking something over, that somewhere there was a higher level of thinking that I hadn't yet reached, that perhaps I wasn't even looking for as yet.

I was conscious of 'explaining away' certain texts of Scripture, such as 'He that committeth sin is of the devil.... Whosoever is born of God doth not commit sin ... he cannot sin, because he is born of God' (1 John 3:8-10). I feared this chapter, with a strange kind of horror. I remember going to a series of Bible studies on the letters of John, and hearing what was no doubt an excellent and scholarly explanation of such passages based on the tenses of the verbs in the original Greek, and so on. Though the interpretation was completely satisfying for the one who taught us, deep inside myself I was not personally convinced. I was frightened of indulging in spiritual dishonesty, of accepting explanations just because they suited me, suited what I wanted to believe, and in this way quieted the qualms of my conscience.

Then again, there were 'expressions' of our faith, certain words and phrases used to express conservative evangelical thought, which doubtless were perfectly accurate and scriptural, but which I suddenly realized had no definite spiritual content for me. I remember so clearly with Olga, in the days which led up to her conversion, how precise she was. 'How do you know it is true?' she would query. 'He is in my heart; He has changed my life', I would reply. 'But how?' 'I received Him as my Saviour; I am cleansed in His blood.' Slowly there entered a gnawing doubt. Was this just evangelical jargon? Was there a reality behind the shadow of words? Olga's conversion became desperately important to me, not only for her own sake, but for mine also. Should she be truly convinced of Him in her head as well as her heart, I would be sure, because I knew that she would not be converted merely through an emotional need (as possibly I had been). And yet at the same time I felt ashamed of this mental attitude of clutching at a straw to convince myself.

It was a method of 'establishing assurance'. Assurance is one of the great glorious truths of the evangelical faith, one of God's great gifts to us from Calvary. Scripture assures us that we may know Him, that we may know that we have eternal life (1 John 5:13). I lacked this assurance as a permanent reality in my life. At one moment I lived in it and enjoyed it, testified to it and taught it to others. Then would come a wave of depression and fears and doubts 'lest that by any means, when I have preached to others, I myself should be a castaway' (1 Cor. 9:27). I had to persuade myself. I had to encourage others to persuade me. I had been baptized as a public committal and testimony, a burning-of-my-boats. It was to me an act of obedience, but it was all part of my effort to receive assurance. I claimed the promises of Scripture, 'He that hath the Son, hath life', 'Lo, I am with you always.' I underlined them in my Bible. These were the facts on which my assurance stood, and still I lacked it as a consistent permanent experience. I accused myself of trying to work up what could only come down from above.

Again there was a certain 'exclusiveness' in the outlook of many Christians I knew that an inner voice urged me to question, the attitude that this was the truth and there was no other. One part of me accepted this utterly. I was deeply convinced mentally of the absolute reality of the truth and value of the Scriptures. But beyond this, I was not so sure. How much was tradition? The phraseology that we used to express the truth—was it not too small to include the whole greatness of truth? Was it not possible that others, though using such different phraseology, were actually describing the same truth? I had experienced a tremendous sense of liberation when He revealed Himself to me. I left the Anglo-Catholic way of worship. I felt the terminology of the mass and of consubstantiation was unscriptural and sadly misleading for hungry souls who were seeking Him who by His own blood 'entered in once into the holy place, having obtained eternal redemption for us' (Heb. 9:12). And yet, as I looked at the life of Father Charles, humble, gracious, consistent, severe and yet withal gentle, he revealed Christ to me. How was this reconcilable?

Another growing fear was that of excusing behaviour with which I knew I ought to be dissatisfied. I suppose this was the outcome of various conflicting doctrines. On the one hand, there was the grand sublime teaching of our eternal security, of our assurance that He who had undoubtedly saved me on Calvary would equally certainly perfect the work and bring me into His eternal presence; that He who had caused me to be born again, adopting me into His family, had promised never to forsake me, never to cast me out, never to loose me from His hand. All this was of grace, infinite wonderful grace, received by faith but never won by works. Yet on the other hand equally, I read that to him who overcame to the end would be given power (Rev. 2:26). To him also was the promise given that his name would not be blotted out of the Book of Life (Rev. 3:5). I read also that there shall in no wise enter into heaven anything that maketh a lie (Rev. 21:27). And there was the story of the unforgiving servant who, although previously forgiven his debt, was delivered over to his tormentors till he should pay every penny (Matt. 18:23-35). Much of the teaching of Scripture was undoubtedly conditional. There were great 'if' passages.

In the mental strain which resulted from all this, I tended to call certain sins weaknesses, or human frailties, and thereby to excuse them. It was nicer to speak of exaggeration, probably due to over-enthusiasm in a good cause, than to speak of lying. Yet I felt I was practising mental dishonesty in making such excuses for myself, and trying to establish assurance. Again, it was nicer to speak of 'warm friendship' than 'inordinate affection', and thus to vindicate the over-exclusiveness of affection between two of us that shut out a third, or at least made her feel uncomfortable and unwanted. It was easy to excuse myself in my own heart with such arguments as 'Surely the friendship could not be sin? Were we not being blessed in witness to others?' Or again, 'Was I not a Christian Union leader, respected and honest, and no-one appeared to criticize my behaviour?'

Then slowly there dawned a sense of exhaustion. The joy and excitement of the first three years suddenly seemed to drain away. When I left Cambridge and started at West London Hospital there was not the same fellowship. There were new temptations and difficulties. Working in a small group instead of in huge classes, I could no longer hide in the crowd and avoid the questions I so dreaded. Work began to get on top of me; unhappiness, loneliness, fear, inferiority, all began to be acutely present. At the same time Bible study and prayer became perfunctory instead of joyous. I no longer wanted Christian fellowship, but had to stir up the desire. Witness continued, but with no real faith or expectation of seeing results. Looking back, it is easy to realize that at least part of the explanation lies in the fact that, like many of my fellow medical students, I was suffering from overwork and strain, resulting from a very full programme. I did not understand this at the time, however, and so thought that this exhaustion meant spiritual failure.

Throughout this difficult period, a coming-down from a mountaintop in order to strike out for another peak, as I could see later, I had a horror of being thought inconsistent. I'll never forget going to Oxford in June 1945 for the Varsity Cricket match. It was to be played on Saturday, but rain caused the match to be postponed. On Sunday morning, on our way to the cricket field, Mary and I met the Rev. W. H. Rowdon, our own vicar from St Paul's, Cambridge, who was the visiting preacher at St Ebbe's that morning! We were carrying our cricket bats over our shoulders. When he stopped to speak to us, asking where we were going, I remember the surprised tone of his voice when he said, 'Playing cricket on a Sunday?' We continued to the match in sober silence. We had given it no thought! We were part of a team, away from home. Could we have let them down overnight? The match started with no joy for us. Oxford women batted first and made 173 for 8. Then Cambridge, believe it or not, were all out for under 30. I was opening batsman and carried my bat for a duck! But my heaviness and dissatisfaction of heart had nothing to do with the score. Were we wrong? Others inferred we were. I must be personally convinced. Was God telling me not to play games on a Sunday? Ironically, I remembered my school days when, as an Anglo-Catholic, I refused to take part in House sports on Ascension Day, taking a lone stand against much determined opposition. Was I not willing to take the same stand now for love of my Saviour as I then took out of reverence for my God?

All these gnawing problems, and the sense of possible dishonesty, led to an almost desperate effort to convince myself. Olga's conversion had been a tremendous buttress to my faith, but could it still be possible that it was all emotionalism, a myth, a soporific? Could it all be untrue? I was urgently aware that I must know the answer, one way or another. I daren't ask openly. I was afraid others might think as I thought, and my questioning might undermine their faith. If one started to question, might it be the start of a snowball, till the whole fabric of faith was shaken?

So the determination grew to teach others, and in this way to convince myself! I threw myself wholeheartedly into summer camps: Varsity and Public Schools in 1947, Inter-Schools 1948, Barbican Mission to Jews 1949, and so on. On Sundays I became a Girl Crusader leader. I loved it. We had our class at home where I was living while studying at the West London Hospital, in a room behind the garage.

Two boy Crusaders came in one week to help me cement the floor and clean the place up. Next week, two or three of the thirteen-year-old girls came and helped me paint the doors and windows. Then we made forms and a table, using sawn logs for the legs. We drew and painted big thermometer-charts for our inter-group class competitions. Days were full and the girls were as keen as I was. The preparation involved for the regular weekly class was good for me.

One Sunday, arriving a quarter of an hour before class, I overheard two twelve-year-olds earnestly discussing the pros and cons of cinema-going. A great yearning grew in my heart not to fail these youngsters, and so our 'Keenite Class' came into being. My only free afternoon was Saturday, so it was given out that any twelve to fourteen-year olds who would like to do regular Bible study could come to my home on Saturday from 3 to 4 p.m. Some of the other leaders were sceptical—Saturday afternoon for a Bible study? But they came! They crowded our small room! I can see them now. The twins, the one thin and wiry, the other round and cosy; Jean, bright-eyed and keen; two little scraps, probably only elevens. Each week anything from eight to sixteen of them would turn up. We set out on the Minor Prophets! I have never learnt so much about the prophets as through those weekly classes—their historical order and setting, spiritual content and purpose, personal application and reality. I loved teaching those youngsters. And yet there was still a haunting fear that I was not willing to be weighed up by my own standards.

Ward services in the West London Hospital were another outlet. There was no nurses' Christian Union at the hospital then—we started one a year later—and there was little fellowship in witness. I obtained permission from the Board and Matron and the Chaplain to conduct these services, covering three or four wards each Sunday. I didn't really believe I would see conversions. It was an act of duty, the kind of thing a Christian medical student should do. I carried a little portable harmonium, set it up in a ward and gave out hymn sheets I had bought. Then, playing with two fingers as best I could, I sang a solo (because no-one sang with me!),

I led in prayer, read from the Bible and preached a short message. Then gathering up the hymn sheets and folding up the harmonium, I would move on to another ward. I spent two hours doing this every Sunday evening for almost three years, constrained by a 'must', a deep personal challenge to fulfil this duty even though at times it was an unpleasant one. Others joined me in this service: a fellow student, Pauline Bousquet, our Casualty Officer, Derek Rose, and at times people from my home church.

There came the day when I accepted the challenge to go to the men's wards as well as the women's. I started in the men's orthopaedic ward. What a mistake! The occupants were sixteen fit and healthy young fellows, some with their legs strapped up in the air following a motor-cycle accident, and others of similar kind. 'What hymn shall we start with?' I never made that mistake again! 'Roll out the barrel', from the far end of the ward! I gallantly plodded through No. 7, 'Fight the good fight', whilst they lustily roared 'Roll out the barrel'. In the second verse, a boot landed on the harmonium. Through the third verse I prayed earnestly what I should do, especially with regard to the boot! At the end of the verse, I picked up the boot and hurled it back down the ward. I didn't play cricket for Cambridge for nothing! The fellows were so impressed that a mere girl could chuck straight, I had no further trouble at all. They all listened quietly, even intently. And then the thrill; after the service one young lad in his early twenties gave his heart to the Lord! My first known convert in those ward services. It challenged me deeply. Why had I not seen others? Why did I not expect conversions? My coward heart answered hesitatingly, because your life does not measure up to Scripture, 'Be ye holy; for I am holy.'

It didn't really matter what people thought. It didn't matter what it cost. One just had to be all out for Him. Sometimes there was a sense of desperation in my heart that days were closing in, and it was our responsibility to tell the heedless and careless, the indifferent and the sarcastic, or else their blood might be demanded at our hands. With it all came this tremendous challenge to holiness. We must be holy. I fought against the apparent cost involved, the realization that I must give up anything that got in the way of 'Jesus only'.

In the wards and in front of other doctors I was very conscious of inferiority, or rather a fear of what others thought. This crippling shyness just had to be subdued and overcome by a daily dying to self, by a vigorous painful effort. Yet there was very little success. Almost crushed, and deeply discouraged, I was invited one day by a nurse to accompany her to see a film. I asked no questions. Coming off duty from casualty at 6 p.m. I joined her and we travelled together to Richmond. We arrived at the theatre late and found it packed out. We stood at one of the doors craning our necks and, taking turns to be in front, were able to watch a little. The film was *Three Miles High*, an amazing record of courage and endurance, of magnificence and beauty, of challenge and determination, filmed in the Himalayas on the Tibetan border. It told the story of twenty years of missionary endeavour against tremendous odds. Immediately, something deep within me stretched out to join this team, to throw in my lot with such people. Major Leonard Moules of the Worldwide Evangelization Crusade was showing the film and was at the bookstall afterwards. I hung around till most people had left, and then went to speak to him. We talked and my heart thrilled. He gave me literature and he invited me to his Mission Headquarters. At last we parted and I returned to hospital, but with a new joy, a new certainty, a new challenge.

Then the struggles redoubled! I had been twice to the Keswick Convention. The addresses I heard there had offered me just what I wanted, all that I was striving after, but they didn't show me how to enter into this wonderful full life. It was all there, the challenging ideal of this glorious life of holiness and victory, of purity and of power. But there seemed no way of bridging the gap from my despair to this liberation. I agreed to all that Keswick had offered me. I agreed to all the teaching of Scripture. My whole being acknowledged that this was the truth, but—there was always that 'but'— my heart wasn't involved in it all. Every part of me cried out that there must be heart involvement, communion within this truth. It was quite plain that mental assent without heart involvement was ultimately impossible.

I was filled with a tremendous desire, a great hunger after Him. I must go on at any cost. I no longer cared what it would mean, or what it might involve. I was willing even to leave my home and join in mission life at WEC Headquarters while still a medical student at the West London Hospital. There at Headquarters I lived in a hot-house of spirituality. Students from Emmanuel College, Birkenhead, from Cliff College, from Swansea, Redcliffe and Mount Hermon Bible Colleges surrounded me, all keenly devoted to His service. Talk at meals was largely of the Lord. I listened in also to organized discussions on different doctrinal and theological matters such as the difference between Arminianism and Calvinism, pre- and post-millennialism, foreign and indigenous missionary strategy, and found myself profoundly ignorant. I joined prayer meetings for revival which went on into the small hours, alive and on fire with a passion for souls and the zeal of the Holy Ghost. I watched lives that were real, earnest, separated, that radiated light and warmth and truth. I longed to be fully one of them. I pleaded with the Lord. I trusted and stepped out in faith, claiming the promises. I tried to fulfil every formula that each one testified to in their own experience. And still my heart felt cold. Sin in my life seemed to mock at my endeavour.

Looking back, it is easy to smile at the intensity of feeling and also the excessive introspection. Yet how extremely real it was at the time. I readily grant that chronic introspection of this type can become very unhealthy, mentally as well as spiritually. As has often been said, a carrot cannot grow if it is continually dug up to see how it is getting on. Nervous individuals can make themselves chronically ill by taking their temperature four times a day and noting each little rise and fall. Likewise, persistent introspection can work one up into a highly tense state of spiritual sickness.

I fell into most of the traps possible. I made myself almost ill through my preoccupation with my own holiness, or rather lack of it! It took a long time to recover from that mistake, which need never have been made. Of course, I never can be holy! How simple, when one realizes that the Lord knows me as I am in all my weakness, loves me, and waits to impart Himself, His own holiness, His life, living in me.

Each conviction of sin was good in so far as it led me to trust the only One who can deal with sin. But if the sense of failure only made me more acutely conscious of my own miserable state, it had achieved nothing. The Lord allowed a growing realization of failure in each of the different realms mentioned, in order that He Himself might fill the vacuum. He longed that I would become more preoccupied with Him and less with myself.

# 5

# Trudging On

For four years I had known that there was something wrong with my voice, some trouble in my throat. Where previously I had been a member of various choirs, I was now no longer able to sing in tune. There was a growing huskiness, a feeling of a 'potato in my throat', accompanied by a slight difficulty in swallowing. I was vaguely afraid, but did not seek advice. Now rapidly the condition worsened, and it became virtually impossible to speak above a strained hoarse whisper. At times I was reduced to using a pencil and paper when I wanted to converse. In March 1950, I entered my own hospital where I was a student for an operation under the ENT specialist for 'benign nodes on the vocal chords'. I was given a small single room adjoining the women's ward. When I came round from the anaesthetic that Friday evening, the walls were cheerfully panelled with large amusing diagrams of the war-time celebrity and such slogans as, 'Wot! No talking?'

An attendant nurse hastened to impress on me that on no account must I make any attempt to speak. Anything I wanted must be written down. The vocal chords must be completely at rest for four days following the operation.

The Tuesday following, while I was alone and resting, a wonderful thing happened. Slowly, an intense awareness developed. Someone was with me. My heart thrilled; the room seemed charged with His presence; a great sense of light was borne in upon me. For two or three hours I was deeply aware of a wonderful companion spirit, not hearing anything, nor seeing anything, but just knowing.

Later, lunch was brought in. The vision dimmed, and yet something had occurred, a new start had been made. From that morning, a hatred of sin was born. Till then I had hated the consequence of sin, the shame of failure, the fear of exposure. But somehow I lacked a hatred for the sin itself. In fact there was a curious liking for it; in its way it was pleasurable. I wished to be freed, and yet I wanted to enjoy it. Suddenly I now knew an intense hatred of all that had crucified my Lord. It was the turning-point for me. The downward path from the peak of happiness, with its puzzlements and questionings, was arrested. Suddenly the next peak stood out clearly ahead. The encircling mist had lifted and left the way clear and inviting. He who was calling me on to service overseas was standing there, gently smiling, promising His presence and companionship and enabling, telling me to look forward and upward, not backward or inward. Suddenly the months of struggle and longing were over, I was satisfied. Not that my doubts were exactly explained; they no longer seemed to need explanation.

The next day the surgeon visited me. He stood at the foot of the bed and commanded me to speak. I had been longing to do so for five days but now found nothing to say! The moment was deeply important to me. Could I speak? At last, fearfully, expectantly, I tried. A deep wave of disappointment and nausea swept over me as I made a noise like the barking of a dog. He examined me carefully, and then curtly said that the operation appeared to have been a failure, but that if I liked to come back in six months he would see if he could help me. With that he left the room; the sister and nurse followed him. I was alone, deeply alone. A wave of giddiness, darkness, heart-ache, came over me. My medical career, let alone my missionary career, was in the balance. My head reeled under the cruel blow. Stunned, miserable, I just lay, tasting the bitterness of the empty future, the mockery of all that had led up to that moment.

Slowly another voice began to force itself through the night in my heart. 'Can you not trust Me?' it seemed to whisper.

'Did I not meet with you only yesterday, beckoning you on to Myself? Why are you so fearful?'

My heart rebelled. Was I not crushed, unable?

'Have you not used your voice for your own ends, for your own glorification, for years? I will give you a new voice for use in My service.'

I just lay there quietly, and slowly peace filtered back into my heart. I felt that His promise was not only with regard to my natural voice; that was just a kind of token. It was to be my whole life, my inability to be holy, my longing after Him—all this He was promising to indwell and fulfil.

That Friday I went home. It was Good Friday, and my mother's birthday. Roughly speaking, my condition was much the same as when I entered hospital. When I spoke it was in a strained hoarse whisper. In the evening of Easter Sunday I went to church with my sister. The Rev. Tom Darlington (who was a missionary in China during the Boxer Revolution) was preaching. It was a powerful sermon, appealing to us to let God the Holy Spirit have His way in our lives, taking possession, infilling, making holy with His holiness. Afterwards a group of my old friends gathered outside the church, discontented and unsatisfied. One challenged me directly: 'Helen, do you know what Mr Darlington was preaching about in your own experience? Is this really something for us now, or only in old age after years of suffering and trial, such as he himself has gone through?' Clearly, without a moment's hesitation, I said a joyous 'Yes!' ringing with assurance. And suddenly I realized He had healed! An amazed hush entered my heart, a tremendous feeling of awe. He had touched me. I looked forward, upward to Him from that moment, and knew that I must always go upwards and onwards, whatever happened in the world around. His call was to live always unto Him.

Six months later I went to see the specialist in outpatients. He was honestly amazed when he first examined me and asked if I had been treated elsewhere. I assured him that I had not sought help at any other hospital, and I tried to testify to him of the power of God to heal. However he merely commented that such cases were known, on occasion, to show considerable regression, and the matter was closed.

Finals followed in three months. What a grind it was! Parts I and II of my final MB comprised some twenty examinations-papers, practicals, orals-a fortnight's gruelling nightmare. The results were read out a short while after I had left my last oral, and though I had passed Part I, I had failed Part II. It was a blow and disappointment, and yet there was the certainty that in six months I would try again and by His grace succeed. So I began a six months' 'trial of endurance', studying all hours, from an early 6 a.m. rise until after midnight. Harry and Gladys Jones came home from Congo that autumn. Mr Jones needed immediate surgery for a large gastric ulcer and came back to us at Mission Headquarters for post-operative care. About this time, his wife developed bilateral pneumonia. I had the privilege of caring for them and spent many hours in their room. We talked much about the work which they had had to leave and that was the start of my knowledge of the need of the Congolese.

The day came to go again to Cambridge for Part II finals. We read Isaiah 58 in the early morning, the chapter of my missionary call, especially verses 6-11. I remember Harry taking up verses 13 and 14 and praying that I would keep holy the Sabbath day in the coming week, and that He would cause me to rejoice in Him as a result. This time He crowned the effort with success. What a thrill, ringing home to say I was through! A doctor!

There followed ten days' wonderful holiday at a Christian guest house near Bournemouth where the Joneses were now recuperating. There was a Salvationist there, an elderly man, I remember, and he had no jersey! I knitted him one, incorporating the Salvation Army badge of Blood and Fire. I gave it to him as a New Year gift, but really it was a 'thank-you' to the Lord for seeing me thus far.

Harry, Gladys and I had wonderful times of prayer and Bible study together, as well as many walks and discussions. It was a time when I could think over many questions that had been shelved during the years of intensive study. Gladys Jones was a trained church worker. Together we discussed and prayed over many problems, particularly such matters as hurtful friendships, inordinate affections, the loneliness of the single woman missionary, and the battles involved in this loneliness.

On 15th January 1951, I returned to WEC Headquarters as a candidate! I really felt I was getting somewhere at last. It was Monday when I arrived, and I moved into one of the rooms on the first floor of the hostel, sharing it with another candidate, a girl from Sweden. On Tuesday, after breakfast and washing up, I was told to go and wash the cement floor of the toilets and bathroom on the women candidates' floor. I found a bucket and brush, and set to. Strange as it may sound, it was almost the first time in my life that I had done a household chore. I was always the trainee-doctor till that moment! I scrubbed out the first toilet and started on the second. A candidate entered the first with muddy shoes. The floor was still wet. When she left, I returned and did the first again. Meanwhile, someone else entered the second. This continued for some little time with a rising sense of frustration. I'd never get them clean! I'd fail, my very first day in training, to achieve the task I was set. Tears pricked at my eyes. I scrubbed on, muttering, 'Devil, get out of here! Devil, get out of here!'

Someone came in, and standing still a moment watching me, heard my muttered comments. She laughed and startled me. 'Now I understand why our cakes are all burnt today!' she exclaimed. 'We're in the kitchen underneath, and you're sending the devil down to us!' She left amused. But there was another quiet spectator, Elizabeth, who was in charge of the candidates and who had given me this task. After a short pause, she gently asked me why I was so upset. I explained the cause of my frustration. 'For whom are you scrubbing this floor?' she replied. 'Why, for you, of course; you sent me here.' I've never forgotten her answer. 'No, my dear. If you are doing it for me, you may as well go home. You'll never satisfy me. You're doing it for the Lord, and He saw the first time you cleaned it. That now is tomorrow's dirt.' It was quiet, godly wisdom that has followed me through many years in Congo.

My six months at Mission Headquarters were wonderful days! Early morning rising at 6 a.m.; serving tea to missionaries on furlough; a quiet hour of prayer and Bible study; breakfast and washing up; family devotions, worship and prayer until 10.30 a.m.; coffee; then 'chores' till high tea at 5.30 p.m.; and those amazing thrilling evening meetings when I learnt what prayer meant, labouring, believing, claiming, rejoicing—all across the world from Colombia to the Philippines, holding on for missionaries and nationals, governments and projects, in persecutions and triumphs. They were tremendous meetings! And so to bed by 9.30 p.m., worn-out and happy.

Chores! What memories there are! I was put in the laundry for most of my six months with Ruth, a grand girl who had just completed her course at the WEC Missionary Training College in Glasgow. Elizabeth showed me the first day what was expected—through the bath (soaking), to the boiler (boiling), to a tub (rinsing), up through the mangle (beware of your fingers!), out on the lines (beware of the mud!), back through the rollers, and so, neatly piled, into the airing cupboards—some thirty-six sheets, pillowcases and towels plus white overalls and the men's shirts for the first day. Starching of collars was an interesting extra! Somewhat fearfully, yet believing for the best, I made a start (merely adding my own personal laundry to the vast pile, to save time) and went through the exercise exactly as instructed. A distracted Elizabeth arrived somewhere around 3 p.m. when all the sheets, etc., were nicely out on the lines in the back garden. 'What have you done?' I glanced round fearfully wondering if I'd set the house on fire inadvertently. 'Everything is green!' I learnt that you don't mix coloureds and whites—the only white articles at the end of my first day were my green ankle socks, shrunk to child's size with happy boiling!

Ruth and I soon discovered how to work the rollers with a minimum of effort. She fed the clean sheets in, and they passed out on to a board balanced on my outstretched legs as I perched on the table, reading aloud to her—always from the very best books in the WEC library!

I was tried for one week in the kitchen, but that was disastrous. Saltless solid lumps floated in a tasteless soup served up as porridge; Welsh rarebit came out like chewing gum surmounted by a sickly yellow sauce. The male candidates could stand no more, and despite grumbles of a 'stiff-necked people' (from over-starched collars) I was duly returned to the laundry.

Norman Grubb, our home-base leader, had recently visited Ruanda and the work of the Church Missionary Society and came home deeply moved of the Spirit at the work of revival he had witnessed there. He spoke many times in morning prayers of the way of the cross, not only for conversion, for the start of our walk, but also for the daily continuance of that walk: 'keeping short accounts with God', the immediate confession of sin, as soon as the conviction registered, listening to the still small voice of the Spirit; the quick claiming of the cleansing of Christ's blood and renewal through forgiveness; the restitution to any offended brother; the joy and happiness of 'walking in the light'. My heart was stirred. I wanted all God had for me. With this renewed desire for close, continuous fellowship with the Lord came an increased sensitiveness towards sin. I began to feel the sinfulness of pride and selfishness and lack of prayer burden, as well as of exaggeration, or deceit, or quick-temperedness. The open way of sharing and fellowship became precious and vital. The candidates were brought into an even deeper unity and joy.

Whilst staying as a student at Headquarters I had made a deep friendship with another girl candidate. We were drawn very close to one another. The urge of affection grew. I found myself hurrying home from hospital to be with her. Then slowly I knew that I was on a slippery path that I had walked before; a demanding friendship that did not want a third person to share it with us. I can thank God now that there were faithful senior friends on the staff who understood, and who separated us. Then the other left for the Far East. I saw her off, and a great blank filled my life for weeks.

Now that I was a candidate my face was set to join her in her missionary sphere. I had been at Headquarters only ten weeks when the staff clearly and firmly told me I could not be accepted for that field. I understood, and thank God, by His loving grace, I agreed and knew that they were right. Then where was it to be? I was a qualified doctor, I was living in a missionary training school. But so far I had no knowledge of where He wished me to serve. Every week missionaries on furlough from any of thirty different countries pleaded for more workers, and almost all of them added, 'specially we need a doctor'. The need was on every side. I could see it clearly! I longed to serve, in turn, in at least six different places. But how could I be sure which it should be?

Daily I asked the Lord for clear guidance, for a definite word from Himself. One Tuesday in April 1951, I tore off the block calendar in the dining-hall and was puzzled by the text there: 'Repair the house of the Lord' (2 Chron. 24:4; 34:8). Why had this been chosen? I pushed the slip of paper in my pocket and forgot it. On Thursday I received a letter from an old school friend (who had been converted in recent years, a fact of which I was unaware). She enclosed that same tear-off calendar slip saying that the Lord had urged her to send it to me. Amazed, I went and read carefully through those relevant chapters but still could not see what the Lord was saying to me. On the Friday at morning Prayers, the leader of the leprosy crusade of our Mission read that same verse, from the same calendar slip, telling us how the Lord had burdened her through it in special prayer for Congo, our oldest field in the Mission, with over 1,500 leprosy patients in our care, and over a quarter of a million Congolese looking to us as a Mission for their medical care, as well as for spiritual and educational help. And yet, after thirty years of pioneer work and earnest prayer, we still had no doctor to offer them. Surely this lack was as a 'breach' in the wall of the church of God in Congo, and He needed us to be burdened to 'repair the house of the Lord'.

I could not get away from it. Three times in one week the Lord had spoken. But I did not want to hear. Not Congo, Lord! Anywhere else but there. But I'm an evangelist, a preacher, a pioneer. I want to go to a people who have never yet heard the message of salvation. Congo is an established church, a ministry to Christians.

On Sunday, as I made my way to my own home church, I prayed again earnestly that He would speak so certainly that I could not be mistaken. The vicar read the story of Balaam and his ass (Num. 22) and he preached on verses 31 to 33! 'Three times the Lord has clearly spoken to you', he said. 'But you do not want to heed. You want something special and dramatic. Beware! He may not be patient for ever. Heed his voice in His thrice-repeated message and obey, and He will bless.' I went home very soberly, but completely convinced that He would have me to serve in Congo.

On 27th June the Mission quarterly staff meeting was taking place. Amongst much other business five candidates were being considered for acceptance into the Mission. I was called to the kitchen, and asked to carry some fifty cups and saucers to the hall next to the library where they were meeting. The swing door into the hall was stiff and heavy. Gingerly I leant on it, pressing, balancing the heavy tray. Very slowly I edged my way in, and carefully along the narrow hall. Suddenly I realized that I was overhearing the staff meeting. I could not hurry! I tried to close my ears, but inevitably I listened for two long agonized minutes to myself being discussed. Lowering the tray on to the table, I fled-back down to my beloved laundry, my face scarlet with shame as I realized what others thought of me—proud, always knowing better than others, unable to be told things or warned or criticized, difficult to live with, and so on.

I carried a basket of sixteen sheets upstairs and hung them on the eight lines criss-crossing the garden. Turning to walk back for another load, I heard a sharp twang. Swinging round dismayed, I saw my precious day's work lying bedraggled in the mud. Suddenly the Lord showed me the funny side of it, and with a rush of laughter, I said aloud, 'Hallelujah!' Those in the staff meeting had seen the disaster from the library windows and had come hurrying out to help. They were suddenly arrested and puzzled, as they heard my exclamation followed by a chuckle of dry humour. It was infectious, and grins slowly spread from face to face. When they returned to their discussions my fate was sealed. I was accepted, a sense of humour being considered heavier in the positive balance than all else in the negative!

That morning my Scripture Union reading had been Psalm 60. Verse 2 had gone straight to my heart, 'heal the breaches thereof'. It was the same phrase! Called into the august presence (the meeting consisted of all missionaries who were then on furlough, together with the home staff, about forty of them all told) I was asked if I had any special Scripture to read first. Asking for Isaiah 58:1-11, I was suddenly shaken, as the reader went on and read also verse 12, 'Thou shalt be called, The repairer of the breach.' After various questions, and loving exhortations and warning, I was given the right hand of fellowship to become a member of the mission.

I had a short holiday, and in September sailed for Belgium to learn French at the Colonial School in Brussels to be followed by a course in tropical medicine at the Medical School in Antwerp. They were eight memorable months. The very first day, knowing practically no French at all, I attended a dictation, with about 140 other missionaries, designed to divide the class into two groups. I understood nothing at all of what was read to us, but wrote down the sounds as best I could. We duly heard the results, and I was listed in the 'forte' class (the strong ones!), presumably because seventy folk, wishing to be in the 'faible' class, had handed in blank sheets. I attended our first lecture without understanding a single word, till suddenly I heard my own name! My neighbour told me to stand up, and then everything seemed to happen till I was in tears, the lecturer shouting in fury, and the class torn between sympathy and amusement! Never mind, that Professor taught me French in four gruelling months, and I can never be too thankful.

In Antwerp, there were more lessons to be learnt. I lived with our missionaries, Mr and Mrs Boerop, and what an atmosphere of sacrificial love there was! I had three weeks in bed with jaundice, following a savage dog-bite when cycling home from school one day. They couldn't do too much for me. Then I followed it with mumps! Their kindly concern knew no bounds. Their teenage daughter Joke and I shared a room, which by day became dining-cum-sitting room. Their boy, now a missionary in Europe, helped his Dad in a hundred and one jobs about the house, and in the Bible shop in the front room.

Then Joke became very ill. There was no extra money available. They trusted me to care for her. Two other missionary doctors on the tropical course kindly came and visited her also, giving their services freely. It was an anxious ten days, of high, swinging fever, interludes of delirium, much pain and increasing weakness. She needed penicillin, but we had no ready money available. All extra money had been spent on me during my four weeks of sickness. We were down to 'brown bread and sugar' meals. Urgently, importunate prayer was made. Each injection of penicillin was 'prayed-in' individually, being provided by the local chemist only as we produced the necessary francs. Yet all the time there was money in the shop from the sale of Bibles. I was puzzled; my faith was sorely tried. Their radiant quiet confidence and unswerving loyalty to principle, and through this, to their Lord and Saviour, was a tremendous lesson to me. Joke got better. My course ended. I left their home deeply-blessed spiritually by their faithful sacrificial fellowship throughout those six months.

Deputation work followed for three months, then a round of farewells to friends and family. There had been a most generous response in many meetings that enabled me to buy the necessary personal needs and medical equipment for the years ahead. Shopping, packing, labelling; visits to consul and shipping agents; vaccination and inoculations; the time passed all too quickly.

And so the great day dawned! I remember at the evening fellowship at Headquarters, Thursday, 12th February 1953, giving my testimony and thanking the staff for 'putting up with me' for the past three and a half years. This was greeted with a resounding 'So you should!' which put me right off, so that I couldn't say any more. The following morning, Friday the 13th, saw me off at Liverpool Street Station at

9 a.m. to catch the boat train to the London docks. I recall the great crowd of staff and candidates on the platform, the last 'phone call to Mother to say goodbye, the accordions and hymn singing, the handshakes and tears. Then the whistle, the green flag, and we're off!

# 6

# Made It!

The Dunnottar Castle sailed late, leaving early next morning as dawn broke over the grey mist of London dockyards. There were seven of us in our party which consisted of two returning missionary couples going out for their third or fourth term of service, an American and his wife from the home base setting off for a six-month tour of our African fields, and myself. With morning Bible studies and prayers, hours spent happily in language study, writing letters and reading, and informal Bible studies with interested passengers in the evenings (the newly appointed Bishop of Kampala led us through the Epistle to the Romans), our days were happily full, as we steamed through the straits of Gibraltar, to Genoa, along the length of Italy, across the Mediterranean to the Suez Canal, in ever-growing heat to Aden, and at last to Mombasa, in Kenya.

The journey had various highlights—principally the excitement as we rounded the easternmost point of Africa. A radio message requested us to change course to due south, instead of south-west, following the coast. A sick sailor on an oil-tanker needed urgent medical care and we were the nearest ship carrying a doctor. We steamed steadily south to the Equator and next day met the tanker. We all watched the short, early-morning drama of the visit of our doctor in one of the lifeboats, and his return with the sick man suffering from appendicitis. Then our steamer began a large swing to steam westwards for Mombasa. Suddenly, the note of the engines changed, and there was another alteration of course. All on deck waited to know the reason. Eventually we spotted a white fleck on the horizon: we steamed slowly towards it and then watched, fascinated, the real drama as several men were rescued. Now in the last stages of despair and agonized thirst, they had been adrift from the Seychelles Islands in a small fishing boat with no stores, compass, or sail, for over nine days. Had we not gone off-course for the oil-tanker, no ship was likely to have seen that tiny distress-signal shirt, and those men must all have perished. How wonderful are the ways of God, directing a great liner carrying hundreds of passengers to the very spot in the ocean where nine pathetic men so urgently needed help! The hearts of all of us were strangely moved that day as once again we swung westward and steamed for Mombasa.

Africa! Customs formalities, unbearable heat, arguments and noise, flies and thirst and at last the train for Nairobi. We had a carriage to ourselves, three double-bunk bed compartments, and one large four-bunk compartment for me and all our luggage. Excitement? I couldn't eat or talk. I was barely able to think for it! I rushed from side to side of the compartment so as not to miss anything. At each station on the long slow climb up from sea-level to 5,000 feet, I leapt down to stand on African soil, to read the name of the station and its height, to sense the feeling of Africa, its smells, and ways, and moods.

We spent a week in Nairobi at the Church Missionary Society's guest house, and for the first time the realization of fear—in those days it was fear of the Mau-Mau. No-one was sure who was friend, who foe. Even a faithful, willing house-boy might have been forced to take the bloodoath, and your life might be in danger.

Up country again to Namasagali, then the lake steamer to Masindi. The heat and dust, the gorgeous frangipani flowers, the leisurely pace, and the horror of seeing someone's precious tea-chest containing a china dinner service haphazardly and unconcernedly tossed from the boat to quay, or quay to boat, with a resounding thud, remain indelibly imprinted on the mind. On again to the edge of Lake Albert. I recall the small steamer, the customs formalities, the happy, indiscriminate mixture of French and Swahili. And so we reached the last lap of the journey. It was stiflingly hot as we crossed the lake, not a breath of wind. Mosquitoes and flies owned the atmosphere, and I felt suffocated under my mosquito net. Out on deck at 5.30 a.m. I watched, straining, for the first glimpses of the Congo as a glorious sunrise broke across the lake, bathing the mountain range in golden crimson light. I was home! It was a deeply thrilling and moving moment, a climax to all that had gone before.

The Mission truck was there. Jack Scholes, my field leader, was at the jetty side, a distinguished-looking man with shining white hair. Beside him were two Africans, and Jim Grainger, his right-hand fellow-worker. They joined us on board for breakfast, everyone full of chatter and news. There were letters of welcome from all the missionaries—almost overwhelming to a newcomer! One from Jessie Scholes to me quoted Zechariah 2:5, 'For I, saith the Lord, will be unto her a wall of fire round about, and will be the glory in the midst of her.'

Customs formalities completed, we loaded up the truck and were off up that tremendous, breath-taking escarpment of countless hairpin bends and magnificent views back over the lake. We stopped at an Africa Inland Mission station for lunch, and what a welcome they gave us! Everyone made me feel I was coming home! Then on again to the Brethren station of Nyankunde, where we were to stay the weekend. There I met two missionaries who had been with me in Belgium. We played some strenuous tennis—not what I had expected in Congo! We arrived at 5 p.m. and that evening an urgent call came for the doctor, but he was away, and I was asked if I would care to go. As we approached the distant forest village we heard the awful death-wailing. We entered the round mud hut, circling between the outer and inner wall in growing darkness, our eyes smarting from the wood smoke, till we reached the centre. Slowly we became accustomed to the dark and the noise, and I knelt beside the still figure, stretched on the earthen floor, already chilling and stiffening, surrounded by naked women (his wives and relatives) rocking to and fro on their heels, wailing abysmally.

After a weekend of rest and fellowship, we set off again. Five of us went with Mr Scholes in the two-ton lorry, and two with Mr Grainger in a three-quarter-ton pick-up. Down from the mountains and wide-open grasslands we drove, into the endless forests, crossing rivers, passing village clearings, on and on, two days of travel, till we reached Ibambi as dusk fell on Tuesday evening, 17th March 1953. My reading that morning had been in Genesis 35: 'Arise... go up to Bethel and dwell there.' Truly I felt this was my Bethel and, like Jacob of old, my one desire was to make an altar there to God for worship and service.

Trees were decorated in welcome. There was even a floral arch as we approached the home up the long avenue of palms—a red banner with cotton-wool words 'Welcome to Ibambi'. We were surrounded by a great and growing crowd of Africans and whites. I remember the talk and noise, the laughter and singing. First to greet us came Jessie Scholes, with her 'Welcome home, dear'. Then Pasteur Ndugu, senior elder of the African church, stepped forward to welcome us all, and myself in particular as the 'new' missionary, in the name of the church.

'We, the church of Jesus Christ in Congo, and we, her elders, welcome you, our child, into our midst.' I never forgot that moment, or those words. What a privilege for a young missionary to be 'their child', one of them, to be cared for, nurtured, loved and taught by them.

Everything was so new, so strange, so exciting. The early morning tea at 5.10 a.m. so as to be able to be ready to go over to the Bible School for morning prayers at 6.30 a.m.; those wonderful morning Bible studies (that term in Hebrews), and the struggle to get beyond the language barrier, breakfast and family prayers followed, and at 9 a.m. over to the dispensary—an empty room in the old Mission Office building, with cement floor, tin roof, wide verandah and large windows. It had so little equipment, just a camp stool and table, some tea-chests with boards across as shelves, a handful of basic medicines, and a few slips of paper hurriedly torn up from an exercise book for report cards. We had no common language but made up for it with an abundance of goodwill. And suddenly there were swarms of patients! Noise, heat, smells, waves of nausea, everyone talking at once, crying babies, running sores...it was dusk before all had drifted away, and I was left cleaning the room, sorting out what there was of drugs, frantically making lists of what we urgently needed, almost overcome by waves of weariness and in the background a slight dread of inability to cope. Then came supper, family Bible study and prayers, cocoa, and so to bed about 10 p.m.

So began the routine, at first with no helper, Congolese or European. But it was a beginning. The Scholes were thrilled, as I was, in the vision the Lord began to unfold, even in those early days, and did all they could to help and encourage me in what seemed a monumental task, the creating of an official and efficient medical service for the church in our 'Heart of Africa Mission' area.

One day that first month there was an evening call to go to see a catechist, Abamangi. Jack Scholes kindly drove me out to the village, some twelve miles off the main road. As we went he talked to me of Mission ways, of the Lord's dealings, of the possibilities of success as a missionary. 'If you think you have come to the mission field because you are a little better than others, or as the cream of your church, or because of your medical degree, or for the service you can render the African church, or even for the souls you may see saved, you will fail. Remember, the Lord has only one purpose ultimately for each one of us, to make us more like Jesus. He is interested in your relationship with Himself. Let Him take you and mould you as He will; all the rest will take its rightful place.'

At Easter I went with the Scholes to Poko, 120 miles north, for the weekend conference. I gave my testimony in Swahili! It was my first public attempt to use my new language. After the service, I met Elizabeth Naganimi, a widow of about my own age, a sweet Christian woman with a great desire and longing to serve the Lord. He spoke to her that weekend,

and she soon came to join me as my first helper and close
friend. Oh, the laughs we had in those early days together
as she spoke Bangala and I stumbled through Swahili, and
neither of us understood a word of each other!

Following the conference came four weeks working at
the Red Cross Hospital at Pawa, fourteen miles north of
Ibambi, travelling to and fro daily, learning more of tropical
diseases, their diagnosis and treatment, and the necessary
laboratory work involved. One day, on the rounds, I noticed
a teenage boy dying of tetanus. Dr Kadoner mentioned
that he was from our Mission. I went back after the ward
round and tried to speak to his parents, with my few halting
words of Swahili. When I felt they understood, I laid hands
on the boy's head and prayed (in English!) in the name of
our Lord Jesus Christ for his healing. As I prayed, I felt the
fever leaving him. I was awed, and a little fearful. Next day,
I asked Ida Grainger to go with me and talk to the parents in
Swahili and to pray with them. She did, and learnt that the
boy had slept peacefully all night, without another fit. He
was, of course, receiving all possible treatment and serum,
but it was clear that the Lord had chosen to heal him.

The following week one of our church catechists, an
elderly faithful warrior, was taken to the Pawa hospital
with an obstruction, for an urgent operation. The next day,
when I arrived, I met his two teenage grand-daughters from
our Ibambi girls' school, on the hospital verandah in tears.
Slowly, there and in the ward, I heard their story.

The old man had not had an operation; he was merely
written up for four-hourly sulfonamide therapy. When
the local nurses arrived at 6 p.m. they offered him his pills
in exchange for one of his grand-daughters for that night
(almost all our Congolese nurses are men). 'I'd rather die',
the old man exclaimed, sending his girls away. They had
gone to a neighbouring village, to Christian relatives,
and returned next morning to see their grandfather. I was
shocked and deeply horrified. I called Dr Kadoner to the
bedside, and tried to explain in excited muddled French; but
he shrugged his shoulders as much as to say that he knew
these things went on but had no power to prevent them. 'Is

not this Africa?' Every part of me refused to accept this, and I vowed, God willing, to have a Christian hospital, run by Christian nurses, where all should see and know Christ's love and purity. The old man died next day.

In May, Mrs Scholes was taken ill. I woke at 2 a.m. and heard her husband moving about, and then heard vomiting. I called out quietly to see if he needed help. She was unconscious, with a fever of over 105°. We made up an injection of quinine from crushed tablets and did all we could. By 6 a.m. her temperature was only 96°, but her blood pressure had fallen to within dangerous levels. I stayed with her all through the next three days as we fought first cerebral malaria, then blackwater fever, with intense weakness, hours of semi-consciousness, vomiting and feeding problems. How I longed for a nurse to help me! How very ignorant I felt as a mere doctor when it came to urgent nursing procedures. For two months we nursed her, and cared for her, and slowly watched the Lord heal her and restore her to us. It knit us together in a deep bond of love. From then on they treated me as one of their own children whom they had had to leave at school in England.

We went away together for a two-week period of rest and convalescence during Bible School vacation, south to Bomili (80 miles) and on to Opienge (a further 140 miles). There we met the Revival. How can one ever hope to explain what we saw and experienced of the mighty working of the Holy Spirit? Senior missionaries and African church elders had been praying earnestly for years that the Lord would graciously pour out upon the Congolese church floodwaters of revival in the Holy Spirit; and suddenly the answer was upon us.

At Opienge, we were at first spectators, puzzled, a little afraid and uncertain, as we saw and heard much that was unusual and foreign to us. Slowly He brought to our hearts the peace of conviction that this was of Him, that He was in control. Meetings were alive with a new power, the building was crowded out as never before. Some were shaking violently, others crying out for mercy, yet others singing and praising the Lord. There was much noise.

Humanly speaking, we might have felt it was confusion, yet He revealed that it was Holy Spirit order. Hour after hour, in church, on the compound, at the home, to Africans or to Europeans, men and women were confessing sins, seeking forgiveness and cleansing, going away full of a mighty joy, their faces radiant with new-found peace. Jesus Christ was being glorified. Sin was being put away. Many were being burdened to pray for the unsaved, to go out in teams of witness preaching the gospel. Surely this was never of the devil! God forbid! Only the Holy Spirit glorifies Jesus.

We returned to Ibambi, arriving on Friday afternoon, 27th July. There we heard from the other missionaries that for two weeks an amazing work of repentance had been going on all over the station compound, many being convicted of hidden sin and seeking out Europeans and church elders for advice and counsel, for confession and restitution.

That evening we gathered in the Bible School for the Friday evening fellowship meeting at 7 p.m. Jack Scholes led the meeting. After some hymn singing and a time of prayer, he stood to minister the Word before opening the meeting for testimonies. Almost immediately, a mighty wave of Holy Spirit power swept through the hall. There was a great rush of noise. We looked around amazed, possibly shocked. Then we felt puzzled, even afraid, as we saw apparent confusion. Africans were on their feet, their arms raised above their heads, calling on the name of the Lord. Others were shaking violently and crying out in apparent pain where they sat. Yet others were thrown violently down, across the forms, on the cement floor, yet without physical hurt. Another rushed wildly to the front and threw himself on the ground, crying violently. Some just sat looking round, stupefied. Some children cried, clinging to their mothers. We prayed, and all felt the conviction that this was of God. The Holy Spirit was in control. We must keep our hands off, and let Him work.

Slowly the pattern changed—tears became laughter, crying became singing, shaking of conviction became trembling with joy, as sin was confessed, cleansing claimed through the blood of Christ, and the Spirit took possession. The singing! It was such singing as we had never heard!

The whole congregation was slowly drawn into the rising crescendo of joy. In the small hours of the morning we began to make our ways home. On all sides the singing continued. Others drifted back, drawn to the fellowship, and worship and singing continued all night and all next day. The station was alive with a new thrill of His presence.

In the weeks, and even months, that followed, a great burden of prayer came upon the church, a yearning over sinners and unsaved loved ones. Many saw amazing visions, of heaven and all the glories of His presence, of hell and the great horror of His judgment. All were seized with a sense of urgency in witness. Schoolgirls would go out in small groups before dawn, to testify to Jesus in some outlying village before getting back again for school. Stories were legion of His power, dealing with backsliders, dealing with outsiders, convicting, cleansing, converting. All had a hunger to hear the teaching of the Word, and a joy in testimony. There was no waiting for people to arrive for services; they used to run to church ten minutes or more before time, and start singing! There was no waiting for people to testify; they queued up. Work on the station went ahead and everywhere there was singing. They were tremendously thrilling days.

At the start, the work was mainly amongst Christians who had hidden unconfessed sin in their hearts and lives, secret drinking, hasty tempers, adultery, impure thoughts, prayerlessness or coldness of heart. Many times as these things were laid open and confessed, my own conscience smote me. Were not the same things, certainly coldness, prayerlessness and impatience, present in my own life? Yet I did not then find release and joy. I joined in their joy, but I held myself largely apart from the work of the Spirit. One African confessed to exaggeration leading to untruthfulness, and I left the meeting bewildered and unhappy. I spoke to the Scholes. I confessed my own fear that I too exaggerated, possibly unintentionally, maybe in circular letters, more by what was omitted than by what was actually written. But I did not find peace and joy. My fellow-worker, Elizabeth Naganimi, deeply involved in the Revival, was radiant. Her shining love often rebuked me and I almost feared to be with her. She walked very closely with the Lord.

One day during this time, as the work of the Spirit spread all over our mission field, station after station sending in wonderful reports of His mighty dealings, John Mangadima, a student nurse at the Red Cross Pawa Hospital, arrived at Ibambi. He said simply that God had sent him to work with me in the church medical service. Later we heard of the great blessing he had been in the camp of leprosy patients at Pawa and of his shining testimony to the doctors there that earned him his dismissal. We also learnt of his quiet acceptance of God's ways. Through his testimony at the Government post where he went to have his labour card stamped and endorsed, a woman, Mama Damaris, was converted and brought to repentance and faith in Jesus Christ. She arrived at Ibambi next day with a glowing face. Asked where she came from, she could only say 'Hell'. Who are you? 'A woman from hell.' Where are you going? 'Heaven.' And the woman from hell joined our ranks to become in the years ahead our chief midwife in charge of the Nebobongo maternity unit.

In the three months before Christmas seven other senior schoolboys joined me at Ibambi, all keen to train as nurses. So was born the vision of the nurses' training school. As I toured our large field area, visiting eleven of our fifteen stations, I became more and more convinced that my main ministry must be to train Congolese nurses to run dispensaries and clinics at each station. They would be nurse-evangelists, preaching the gospel to their own people, gathered through their need for medical care and aid. 'Repairer of the breach.' This seemed clearly the meaning of the phrase which had been so prominent in my missionary call, to supply a Congolese medical service to their own people, staffed by keen, well-trained church workers, of a similar standing to the church, Bible-school-trained, evangelists.

In January 1954, we held our missionaries' conference at Ibambi, when all gathered together for prayer, Bible teaching and spiritual refreshment, and to discuss our programme for the coming three years. I looked forward immensely to this gathering, and to meeting all my fellow workers. Yet

I was not unconscious of underground tensions and a sense of anxiety. There were those amongst us who were not in sympathy with the way He had chosen to send and reveal revival power in our midst. There were personality clashes and hidden jealousies. There were determined views on many subjects that seemed not to be in accordance with the general policy.

During the conference, both Dr John Harris, who had arrived in Congo only four months after myself, and I were asked to give some idea of our medical vision and proposed programme. John was keenly interested in the welfare of leprosy patients throughout our area of responsibility. I was keenly interested in the training of national workers to accept this medical responsibility. We outlined our plans; we sought permission to go ahead. Then came the question: Where should the nurses' school be located? It seemed obvious to me (and therefore subconsciously I expected it to be obvious to everyone else!) that it should be at the centre, at Ibambi, where we were already firmly established. So it was a shock to realize that some were strongly opposed to having the medical centre stationed at Ibambi—anywhere else, at all costs! After hours of discussion, it was eventually agreed that it should be in the Ibambi area, but not actually at the station. It was suggested we move it to Nebobongo, seven miles north, where for many years we had had a large camp for leprosy patients and maternity work.

I was somewhat stunned. I felt so sure it was not His will to make the medical centre a separate work from the Mission, under separate administration with all the problems that my quick mind could see clearly following such a move. However, I was encouraged to wait quietly and let the Lord resolve the problem in His own way and time. There was no immediate hurry.

I remember at that conference the wonderful daily Bible studies led by Jack Scholes, from the first eleven chapters of Leviticus on the four 'basic tenets' of the Mission: faith, holiness, sacrifice and fellowship, as revealed in the sacrifices, the types of Calvary. One illustration which he used about a carpenter stands out clearly in my mind today. The man had completed preparations to make a cupboard, each board cut accurately to size, planed and aligned. Now he gathered up nails of various sizes and different heads, for the final assembly. Holes were bored to receive the heads: the nails were placed in position in turn, and then hammered home, covered over with wood filling, and the whole varnished, so that in the completed article no nail was seen, only the cupboard as a whole. Were we willing to be nails, in the hands of the Master Carpenter? Would we grumble at the painful blows of the hammer, or would we remember that the hammer was held by the nail-pierced hands? It was He, not our circumstances, nor our fellow-missionaries, who was choosing us to take our hidden place in His church.

The conference ended; days of tidying up followed; station routine recommenced. Then, on 20th January 1954 our nurses' school started, with a membership of eight. It was a very humble start. I was not fluent at Swahili, and used no French. The boys were from all different standards, from John Mangadima who had done one year post-primary school and was keen to go ahead, to Joseph who had only completed 4th grade primary and been out of school for some years with practically no desire for academic advancement. I had no notes to help me, no idea of what such a course should include, no indication from the Government as to official standards or syllabus.

We built our first two wards, a lovely whitewashed mud building with a thick thatch and large shuttered windows. On one side was a twenty-four-bed ward for women and children, a hall for consultations and drug cupboards, and three small rooms, for maternity, minor surgery or special cases. All these were to the right of our dispensary. On the left, we built a small eight-bed men's ward. The church members did most of the work, helped by nurses and patients. Catechists and evangelists came in to roof it. It was officially opened, named 'Bethany' and dedicated to the Lord's service in September 1954.

One day in this same month I was sitting on my verandah during the lunch-hour rest period when I was presented with a whimpering six-month-old baby, sturdy, healthy, but hungry! The agitated aged relative, who almost threw her at me, told me that her mother had died that morning. They had tried to bring her to me, but were prevented by flood-waters. He pleaded with me to adopt the child, so that she might be brought up to love the Lord. If I refused, her other relatives would take her and she might never hear the gospel, So 'Fibi' (Swahili version of Phoebe, 'moonshine', light reflected from the sun) entered my home and, in a few days, my heart, to become my own little girl. The sudden weaning, linked with my own ignorance of milk mixtures and sugar measures, led us into three dreadful weeks of endless crying, diarrhoea, skin rash, losing weight, and frantic disturbed nights. But slowly we got to know each other, and to enter on our new life together.

I was ill in late November with a severe attack of malaria. Elizabeth Naganimi took little Fibi, and from then on became her nanny, her most precious friend, her faithful tutor in things temporal and spiritual. I had to be at Bomili for Christmas, to attend the confinement of one of our missionaries, although I was hardly fit for the journey. On arrival, I developed jaundice, and an unhappy three weeks followed. So many memories crowd those days. I recall eating a red-hot pepper by mistake; the birth of a white baby in a village surrounded by forest, seventy miles from the nearest hospital should aid be needed. I remember the love of our Ibambi evangelists and their wives, eight families who were working in the Bomili area as missionaries, to help this much smaller church to get established.

So back to Ibambi for another year of work. The nurses' training school was going ahead. Arthur Scott, one of our missionaries who had trained in Belgium as a Health Officer, had sent me the notes he had prepared over the years for training African nurses. These, with Dr Chesterman's textbook for African dispensers, made the basis of our new textbook, painstakingly typed out for each of our eight students each evening for the following day's lectures. Then Miss Roupell, another missionary, became very ill. I drove her to Stanleyville, along three hundred miles of Congo roads, to have an electro-cardiogram and to see a heart specialist. After that we had a tremendous epidemic of infective hepatitis; then another of a severe kind of measles. Days were always full. But God gave the ability to cope with ever-increasing responsibilities. Greek traders brought their children to me with tonsillitis, or for general check-up during their school holidays. Africans poured in from every side, demanding a surgical service, midwifery care, eye specialist work, plus the multitudinous stream of medical cases. The work grew and grew; the vision clarified; I was happy.

In October 1955 five of my nursing students were ready to go for their state examinations. We were all terribly nervous! I managed to provide each of them with new khaki shorts, a shirt, and a clean white apron. I drove them up to Pawa in my Chevrolet van. They were subdued—very strange for Congolese! We were ushered into one of the rooms at the back of the large laboratory buildings where the Red Cross nurses had their schooling. There we were joined by some twelve of their students who were all talking off-handedly in French. Our boys felt awkward, knowing only the local Swahili. But they were the better dressed (small comfort to my heart)! a government doctor came from Wamba, eighty miles to the east, the Red Cross doctors were there, and myself. For their oral examination the boys came in singly, my students politely being offered first place. Each one had from five to fifteen minutes' questioning (in Swahili, I was relieved to hear) while the doctors chatted casually amongst themselves, and seemed to give scant attention to the answers. I dared not look at my boys. I was frightfully anxious they should do well. At last it was over and the results were read out. Yokana of Ibambi was first with 95 per cent! Mangadima was third with 85 per cent; two other Ibambi boys had passed, and one was deferred till next year's exams. It was wonderful news! We set off home, singing triumphantly the whole journey, wild with excitement.

Our medical service for the Congolese church was launched. Our first Africans were qualified as State assistant nurses. We were established! The future looked settled. I went to bed that night, radiantly happy, flushed with success, heady with the first draught of popularity.

# 7

# Further Vistas

Christians often seem to have the impression that 'becoming a missionary' is some form of metamorphosis by which a radical change of nature is achieved. Someone, possibly deeply stirred at a missionary meeting and challenged by the need of some less-privileged people, feels constrained to offer for overseas service. Almost inevitably this 'offering' comes to be regarded as a 'holy call' to a sacrificial vocation. The whole idea becomes wrapped in a veil of romantic splendour, so that even the candidate may fail to observe the unreality of it. The tendency of congregation and friends well-nigh to hero-worship the missionary only increases the dilemma. Looking at the situation honestly and critically, many may know that, mentally, physically or spiritually, the candidate is unsuitable for missionary service. Some would-be candidates do not even have a burden of prayer for the peoples they hope to serve, nor have they ever sought to bring their immediate friends and neighbours in their own country to a knowledge of their Friend and Saviour, Jesus Christ. Yet they vaguely hope that as soon as they board the steamer or plane to take them to a foreign land, something mystical will occur and transform them into their image of a 'missionary'.

Nothing can be further from the truth! I believe that, at its simplest, a missionary is one sent by God to live a Christian life, usually amongst people other than his own. It is living which counts. This may include formal preaching, but it will certainly include personal relationships, and these often have to be worked out under most trying conditions. For example, many missionaries discover that it is far from easy to adapt themselves to a completely different climate. The native foods may be hard, not only on the digestive system, but also on the aesthetic tastes. The language barrier may constitute a difficult problem, especially in early years. One cannot choose one's friends. Two missionaries of vastly differing backgrounds, likes and dislikes, may be thrown together for several years with no choice of other companionship. One is often expected to do jobs for which one is not trained, and which may be actually distasteful. Yet in all this, one is called upon to reveal Christ, to live a Christ-like life, to be a 'missionary'.

It is then that one realizes it is not the journey in the steamer that changes one's nature. I did not escape from myself by going to Congo. Rather, I came to know myself better, perhaps more as others had already seen me. The ordinary trials and frustrations of life that meet us all were just as real in Congo, and, in some ways, were more pronounced, as there were fewer ways of avoiding or circumventing them. For myself, it was only as I allowed the Lord to show me my own pettiness, or wilfulness, or pride, in different circumstances and problems, that I became willing to let the Lord teach me of Himself. 'Take my yoke upon you, and learn of me', the Lord said, 'for I am meek and lowly in heart.' What happened in the two years following my first taste of success as a missionary doctor shows simply how very much I had to learn of Him, for surely no-one merited the description of Christ-likeness less than I, if it was to involve the phrase 'meek and lowly in heart'.

The day after I returned from taking my students to Pawa for their State nursing examination, Jack Scholes came over to the dispensary to see me at midday. He informed me that the Mission field committee, then in session at Ibambi for their quarterly meeting, felt that the time had come to implement the suggestion made the previous year at the field conference that the medical programme of the Mission should be run from Nebobongo. They would like me to make preparations to move there that week.

I felt as though I had been slapped in the face. Stunned by the sudden overwhelming realization of what this decision would involve, battle royal raged in my heart. Standing surrounded by my first achievements—nurses, buildings, outpatients—I envisaged the gruelling task ahead, and resented the apparent thoughtlessness and thanklessness of this demand, coming at this particular moment. Rebellion flared up within me, and I determined to withstand what I felt was a bigoted, even stupid, committee blunder, sure in my own soul that it was totally detrimental to the overall vision of God's will and pattern for the Mission medical service.

Mr Scholes agreed to my impassioned demand that I might come over and see the committee that evening. All day the fire smouldered in my heart. My mind seethed with bitter criticism against the 'committee', unhappy in the certain knowledge that the decision was made, in part at least, because of personal antagonisms. I therefore felt quite justified in arguing that it was not in His will. With the clinics finished, hospital clean, school over, I washed and changed, going over and over what I intended to say. My arguments and proofs were all ready. I thought I knew what they would reply, and I had already planned how I would prove their arguments false. A fellow-missionary who was staying in my home at the time tried to calm me down, but I was in no mood to listen. I went across the compound, seething and unhappy.

I had to wait. Mrs Scholes suggested we pray together. Never! Pray? With my heart aflame and my tongue poised for battle? Impossible! Quietly, she herself knelt and prayed for me out loud. Slowly the fire died out, a hopeless helplessness flooded me, a feeling of 'very small littleness', and I began to see the pointlessness of battle. Then she talked with me, of Jesus, and His deep, deep love. 'He that toucheth you toucheth the apple of his eye' (Zech 2:8). It was not the committee, not a group of fellow-missionaries, but the Lord Himself—through them, it was true—who was sending me to Nebobongo. He had a great purpose, possibly a difficult, even dangerous, way; but He would go with me. At Ibambi He could not do for me what He wanted to do, to make me 'more like Jesus'. It was His hand, His nail-pierced hand, that held the hammer (even the committee!) to fulfil His purpose, to drive the nail fully home to take its place in the building of His church. 'All things work together for good to them that love God, to them who are the called according to his purpose' (Rom. 8:28). When called to the committee, I listened quietly to their proposals and was given the grace to agree. And looking back now, how glad I am that the Lord overruled and constrained me to obey.

On 30th October 1955, I left Ibambi in the Mission truck with all my possessions to go seven miles north to Nebobongo to take over the responsibility of station leadership and the development of a Mission medical service. Evangelist Agoya and his wife Taadi, with their six children, went with me. They had had to return to Ibambi from their work at Bomili after eighteen months' missionary service as Taadi was desperately ill with her sixth pregnancy, and we had grown very close to each other, as sisters in the Lord, during those anxious months.

So started a new life. Mr and Mrs Coleman and their young family had left for furlough the previous week after caring for Nebobongo for a couple of years. I joined Florence Stebbing, a capable nurse and midwife, who had already had some four or five years' service at Nebobongo. The work generally was in a discouraging state. In 1953, the Belgian Red Cross Hospital at Pawa had closed the large and flourishing leprosy colony that Mission nurses had supervised at Nebobongo since 1940, taking over a thousand of the camp family to their own new centre, some nine miles further north. The remaining two hundred patients had scattered to surrounding villages, refusing to be coerced to this Roman Catholic hospital, preferring to forgo treatment. The beautiful colony, with its rows of homes, neatly-laid-out gardens, and flourishing acres of food crops had reverted to jungle. There was almost nothing left to be seen of it. The station workmen, many of them previous camp patients, were drifting away, as Nebobongo was no longer considered a treatment centre. However, the small, neat, brick-built maternity unit, with its ten beds and well-equipped labour ward, continued, due to Florence's constant care and love, staffed by a group of pupil midwives whom she trained with endless patience.

There was also the orphanage, consisting of two long, low, brick buildings, filled with small wooden beds, each with a separate room at one end for the five Christian women who cared for the thirty-eight noisy, happy toddlers! What a sight to see them all in an open verandah, on forms by the low wooden tables, with folded hands and bowed heads singing 'Grace' before the steaming bowls of rice, plantains, and manioc leaf were handed round! They were all ages, from nought to ten, most of them dressed in bright-coloured cotton rompers. Each of the five women carried on her hip, slung from one shoulder, one of the newest arrivals, still bottle-fed.

The station layout was interesting. Our land lay all to the north of the Paulis-Ibambi road, half a mile of road-frontage on a sharp bend. Opposite us, to the south, was forest and dense undergrowth, sloping away down to a stream and marshland. Florence took me on a tour of inspection. We started at the Paulis (eastern) end of the roadway. All the land to our right was cleared, rising from us in a fairly steep embankment to a half-mile-long, flat plateau-top, parallel with the road, 120 yards back, and mostly only about 50 to 70 yards wide before falling away again, plunging downhill at both ends to streams and freshwater springs, and centrally leading away to the old colony for leprosy patients. We left the road by the first entrance, and climbed up to a very nice, almost square, brick-built home with grass thatch roof where Florence was living. It had four rooms, a kitchen and bathroom and, out behind, a cookhouse. Walking along the plateau-top, westwards, we looked down the steep hill to our right to the African workmen's village, some twelve homes, many of them urgently needing repairs or renewal. To our left there was a large mud-hut home where maternity patients waited for their babies, and this house, too, was obviously in very bad repair. Continuing to our right, we passed a lovely church building, low brick walls and pillars, and newly thatched, standing on the rough cement floor of the old home of the founder of the leprosy colony, Mrs Edith Moules, who had started the work at Nebobongo in 1940. The church could seat about eighty to ninety, and was also used for primary schooling for the orphans. A few were in there as we passed, being taught the rudiments of reading, writing and arithmetic by one of the pupil midwives. But one had the impression that teacher did not know much more than those taught, and probably very little was getting across. So we came to the maternity compound, with brick-built, grass thatched buildings for normal and infected cases, and houses for the midwives.

The station was divided into two by the road that ran north-south through the middle, from the main road back to the old leprosy colony. Crossing this, we came to the second large European home, where I was now to be installed—a house with some eight rooms and bathroom, and a verandah. There were no Africans living within hailing distance of either of our homes, our cooks and their families lived down in the village. Opposite my home, across the wide drive, there was a coffee plantation (where today the primary school stands). Further westwards was a large open courtyard, with two long, low dormitories for the orphans, their kitchen, and the open verandah for meals. On again, we came to a long narrow stretch of level wasteland.

We went to inspect the water supplies, scrambling down to the streams through rough undergrowth, along narrow muddy tracks. They were in bad shape, dirty, overgrown, full of insects, the sure source of sickness. We made our way towards the leprosy colony, but all was overgrown. Even the roads were hard to decipher in the new jungle, and we stumbled home not a little discouraged.

That evening, I met the whole family in church for a welcome meeting. We eyed each other speculatively. My mind was full of housing problems, water supplies, feeding, clothing, administration, sanitation, counting how many there were and trying to calculate what it was going to entail. They for their part were wondering if I would stay, whether they were going to have security again and jobs, if I would work in with them or shout at them and throw my weight about. But slowly, together, we thawed out towards one another, and it would seem that we all decided that first evening to trust Him to work it out for us, to unite us as one family and make a success of the new venture.

Next day, with Agoya and two of the senior station workmen, we got down to it. We walked all over the ground a hundred times, with paper and pencil and tape-measure. We drew up plans and discarded them, and started all over again. Eventually, it began to take shape and a new vision crystallized. I sent a message to the church elders responsible for the work in our area, asking them to meet with us and discuss our plans. First, we wanted them to seek out relatives for as many of the orphans as possible, or else Christian friends who would adopt them into their homes, as we felt that to make a start with the hospital, we must take over their buildings and build more around them in that courtyard. Second, we wanted to build a completely new workmen's village in a healthier spot, on the long level stretch of wasteland at the western end of the station. Third, we wanted them to find us a teacher for our children, the orphans who would stay with us, the children of the evangelist and the workmen and the nurses. Fourth, we wanted them to find us a team of eight willing Christian workmen to make bricks down at the old brick-kiln, ready for new hospital buildings.

They agreed, and we all set to with a will clearing land, cleaning water-holes, digging new toilets, planting food gardens. It all took time, and it was a full year before we began to see results for all our labour. We made many mistakes, needless to say: sharpening the teeth of the long double-handed saw without setting them first, for instance; building the firing-holes in the kiln too widely spaced so that they fell in, so losing us 17,000 of our first 22,000 bricks; miscalculating the volume of hewn trees for kiln firewood on the Government return sheets involving us in tremendous expense; building a new dispensary as a roof on pillars only, with no walls, so that it was blown away in the first hurricane storm. But we learnt!

There were more serious mistakes, too. Out of twelve orphan children who were taken home to Christian relatives or adopted into various homes, eight came back to us, unhappy and underfed, and we had to re-think our programme for them. We realized that we could not sacrifice them to the cause of progress in another direction. We were unable to obtain a school teacher for them, so I taught them myself for three hours every morning. But I taught them as I knew how, and when they took exams to go to the central Mission primary school at Ibambi, to pass up from our grade 3 to their grade 4, they all failed. I had used English methods and these were unacceptable in a Belgian colony.

Letters came from other missionaries asking why I couldn't visit their stations, as I was the Mission's doctor, not just Nebobongo's. I regret to say I was annoyed and wrote indignant replies reminding them that they had sent me to Nebo, and pointing out that having, as I did, station responsibility, I was up to my eyes in work—administrative, building, and educational, as well as medical. I urgently needed a chauffeur-mechanic to relieve me of all the endless driving for weekly food-markets, and for emergency patients. One day a young man arrived with his wife and two little boys from the Wamba station, saying he had heard I needed a chauffeur and he wished to offer for the job. We were thrilled! We showed him a house in our new village, and everyone welcomed the family and helped them to settle in. Next day at morning prayers, there was a call for the ambulance. I called Daniel to me, passed him the car keys, named a student nurse to go with him, and gave him the scribbled note of appeal with the address. He just stood and looked at me. Well, I asked, what do you want? I then discovered he had never even sat in a car before! He had come to be taught to be a chauffeur mechanic! He learnt, and I learnt a lot too, in order to teach him! But he became my most valued friend during the next three years and an extremely good chauffeur.

More serious still, I was working almost round the clock. My days began at 5.30 a.m. in the hospital wards, and rarely finished before 10.30 p.m. in the office. In addition, there were frequent night calls, emergencies that broke in upon an already tightly packed programme, operative responsibilities that sorely tried me and left me tired and worn out afterwards. As a direct consequence my quiet times alone with God in the morning, drawing fresh strength and inspiration and guidance, began to peter out. I still did regular Bible study as I taught for three-quarters of an hour every morning in church before the day's work began. But it was becoming automatic. The joy was slipping away. The desire for prayer fellowship with whites or Africans began to fade. One knows how closely physical tiredness and spiritual ill-health are linked, and this tiredness faces so many missionaries who have to cope with the problems of under-staffing and overworking.

Little things began to make me irritable. I remember one day, a Thursday, when I did an eye-clinic in the morning at 9 a.m. I had got the house ready, darkened rooms, instruments out, and two patients came. After they had gone, I waited a little while, had coffee, and then another came. After that, and a further wait, I cleared up everything and prepared to go to the hospital for ward-rounds. At midday an old lady was led to the verandah of my home. My houselad came to tell me that she wanted her eyes tested. I was annoyed and asked where she came from. It was from a nearby village, so I refused to see her, saying she could have been in time for the 9 a.m. clinic and must come back next week. I turned away and went in for my lunch.

Shortly afterwards, my senior dresser, John Mangadima, came to me. He was grieved, and rebuked me for turning the old lady away. 'Could you not see that she was blind? She has waited all morning at the roadside for someone to come to lead her to the Christian doctor who heals people. She is a soul for whom Christ died, and you have harshly turned her away. Would He have done so?' Since then, I have always lifted my heart in a quick, silent prayer as I go to answer the door, that I may receive every visitor, whatever the hour, in His name and for His sake, showing His love and gentle kindliness and courtesy.

Meanwhile the work grew on all sides. We urgently needed extensions in the maternity compound where some forty babies were being born each month and some twelve pupil midwives were in training with three qualified girls in charge. We urgently needed more room in the hospital compound. By this time we had two wards, one with eighteen beds in it for women and children, and one with eight beds for men, yet we often had as many as fifty patients at a time needing hospital care. The out-patients had to be seen on the verandah, sometimes as many as 150 at a time, with nowhere to sit for morning prayers, or for treatments, and no shelter when it rained. The other building, which acted as laboratory, pharmacy, theatre and a place for sundry other 'odd jobs', leaked badly and also needed a damp-course built in.

We had no hospital village for the countless patients who came from far-distant places and needed daily clinic treatments. Our own new station village was growing apace; there were already two neat rows of eight houses each. But the number of student nurses and young workmen grew faster than the village. We had several acres of land under cultivation, with large crops of peanuts and rice, manioc and plantains, paw-paws and pineapples. But still we had to buy nearly one ton of food each week for our ever-growing family. Once again, we had over thirty orphans in our care, but at least two of the women who cared for them were now too old, and really too weak, to continue their work of drawing water, cutting firewood, and endless laundry and ironing, cooking and feeding, as well as mothering and spiritual care.

We now had over thirty children of primary school age in the four first grades, as well as twenty student nurses in the three years of their course; and all the teaching fell on me! The administrative work, involving Government forms, accounts, reports, letters, grew at about the same pace, and yet all had to be done somehow, usually after 10 o'clock in the evening, often with many mistakes made through sheer weariness. But where could one call a halt? To which department could one say 'No'? Everyone had a claim. Needs abounded; our reputation had grown particularly for eye clinics and maternity work and tuberculosis, and patients came to us from as much as 400 miles away. Could we refuse them?

It is easy for Christians at the home base to say that a missionary should not do too much, and should take one day off in seven. In theory, we all agree. But when one is a doctor, single-handed, with no other medical help for 50 or even 150 miles in any direction, it is hard to put into practice. How urgently every missionary society needs new recruits to share the work-load. This would seem to be the only practical solution to this world-wide problem.

Others argue that missions should not tackle institutional work, such as schools and hospitals, but leave these to the Government. In our area, and in many, many others, this would merely mean that thousands of children would have no schooling, and thousands of patients would die each year, as the Government just has not enough skilled and trained servants, nor a sufficiently stable economy, to begin to shoulder the work of this vast responsibility, willing though they may be.

In January 1957, we had another triennial field conference, this time with a difference—our African church elders were to take part with us. The conference was to be bilingual. Bangala and Swahili were to be used for the joint meetings of Africans and Europeans; but other meetings would be held separately to discuss specifically church (African) or Mission (European) matters, bringing together the findings at the next joint meeting. Dr Harris and I both presented medical reports, and then the southern group of churches added an urgent plea concerning their need for a medical service in the south, particularly requesting a general surgical service. After much prayer and discussion it was suggested that Dr Harris should come south from Malingwia to join me at Nebobongo. There he would train me in surgery, and then I would leave him at Nebo, and go south myself to start again a similar work for the churches there.

After the conference had ended, Florence Stebbing went on furlough. John and Elsie Harris joined me at Nebobongo for a brief week, with Joy and Cyril Taylor and their two little boys. Then they all left for their different stations, and I was alone. It was a strange feeling, but I loved it! For one thing, it was a tremendous challenge. Could one cope with the multitudinous tasks alone, and keep all the services going smoothly? By the Lord's strength and enabling, yes! And with it all, I found full scope for such determination and vision and administrative ability as I might have. But I do not doubt that it made me selfish. I had no need to consult with others, nor to consider their desires or feelings. I had no time-table to keep except my own. I had no need to be careful not to over-drive others. I could work at the pace I preferred. My African team worked willingly with me, each in his own department pulling his weight and doing his job, so that the whole machine rolled smoothly on. I felt a great glow of pleasure and pride. But with it there was an uncomfortable pricking of conscience that this was to my glory and not necessarily His. I was proud of them, each one of the big family, and they were mine—my nurses, my workmen, my hospital, my vision. And He had to teach me that they were His.

Ruth Dyer, another woman missionary, joined me for two months to do language study as she was moving from the northern to the southern area of our field, and also to be my companion. We were very happy together, and she helped me tremendously in preparing for the arrival of Dr Harris and his family. There was sandpapering and revarnishing of furniture, doors and windows, painting woodwork, supervising the workmen in distempering the big house. We did each room in a different pastel shade, using methylene blue, mercurochrome, malachtite green and flavine from the dispensary to stir into the baths of whitewash! They looked first-rate, the colours giving it a really professional touch. The Harrises were expected on Tuesday, 2nd May. We killed a chicken and prepared a feast. They didn't come. Ruth left me that week. I thought we must have got the week wrong, so next Tuesday we killed another chicken and prepared another feast. Still they didn't come. The next Tuesday I felt I couldn't go on killing precious chickens, so we did nothing—and they came! On 16th May 1957, just as dusk was falling, they drove in. I was in the hospital with an emergency case—a man had been carried in with a horribly torn foot. As light was failing, and it was nearly supper-time, and I was tired (we can always make lots of excuses!) I hadn't lit the pressure lamps in the hospital, but was working in the half-light on the verandah outside, in most unhygienic conditions, and in a most unmedical manner. The first thing I knew of their arrival was when Dr Harris walked up behind me. I felt my pride fizzle out of me. I was caught doing everything just as one shouldn't do it!

# 8

# Slipping Back

Next day Dr Harris and I walked round the whole site together as I showed him all aspects of the work. At midday we went to his home for family dinner, and I saw that, except beneath the pictures, all our beautiful colours had completely disappeared, bleached out by the sun. And I had a slight premonition that this might be a picture of myself. After lunch we gathered together for prayer and discussion, and to seek for a happy division of labour. In the evening we had fellowship with the church elders and laid before them our suggestions. Thus I officially handed over the leadership of the hospital to Dr Harris.

How hard it came to me! Little had I realized how utterly Nebobongo made up my life, how each workman, each nurse, each child had curled themselves into my heart as part of my family. And now, officially, they were no longer mine. For the next year I fought out this fight, and through it found myself in depths of despair, seeing myself as a failure, useless, realizing that I had built the work around myself, and my personality, and my vision, instead of on Him. Mine was written on everything, instead of His. And how deeply it hurt, as, gently and lovingly, He had to prise my hands off His treasured possession.

There seemed to be endless frustrations. I had grown to love the liberty of leadership, the joy of working a thing out and seeing it through and making a go of it. But now

I was once more just a junior missionary, and my ideas did not always make sense to those working with me. Through the past eighteen months I had learnt a good deal about administration—in my own way! But book-keeping and office work were certainly not my strong points. What the fourteen different books said should be in the fourteen different accounts corresponded to what could be found in the fourteen carefully labelled porridge-oats tins. But how I achieved this was not always so clear! Those who took over from me had somewhat more accurate views and more accurate methods, and doubtless suffered many headaches in sorting out and clarifying many mysterious entries. But it was not by any means easy to accept the very definite change in emphasis regarding financial affairs. I had felt so clearly led through the years in what I called a 'Muller' practice. As God gave a vision, I would seek from Him the tenth part of the needed finance to see the project through, and then launch out in faith, trusting Him for the rest to come in as it was needed. Now I had to toe the line, so to speak, to a very different method of working, though doubtless it was the more usually acceptable. Now we asked the Lord to provide all that was necessary for a project before commencing work on it.

No doubt I was something of a visionary, and all my hard work and labours were working to one end, the fulfilment of a very clear vision of what I felt was Congo's greatest need, particularly in our north-eastern Province. I wanted to see bush clinics every fifteen to twenty miles, looked after by well-trained African dressers, where preventive medicine, child welfare clinics, ante-natal clinics and school-children clinics could form the prominent part of the work, along with the early diagnosis and prompt treatment of all the current endemic diseases, tuberculosis, malnutrition, leprosy, intestinal worms, etc. This could be followed by immediate transference to the centre for any not responding promptly to treatment. I longed to be freed from the central work, so that I could set up and organize, and then regularly visit, clinics such as these. I felt that they would need a fort-nightly oversight at the start. The people of an area would be told what day and time the doctor was expected and could gather at church centres where the local catechist or evangelist would buy up the opportunity with the ministry of the Word of God. I personally had little interest in the hospital routine work, feeling that there were several Government and Red Cross hospitals in the area which these clinics could use, especially for surgery. So the nurses' training school at Nebobongo had developed with this special emphasis, the preparing of young men to carry the responsibilities of bush clinics, both as evangelists and as medical dressers.

Now, however, a change came, and I was not willing to recognize the vision of another if it did not happen to coincide with my own. And what a continual cause of friction in church and Mission this attitude can be! Many in the Mission, and this certainly included the majority on the committee, felt that an established central work with proper surgical facilities was of greater importance than a string of 'inefficient clinics'. If I must travel, they said, why not tour the Mission stations, and help the other European nurses who were struggling to keep small hospitals and maternities going throughout our area with very little outside medical help or encouragement? Under pressure, I agreed to do a six-monthly tour of the stations, involving a five hundred miles' circle to the south and a similar circle to the north, in a huge figure of eight. But our vehicle was old and not really road worthy; the roads were shocking, and the first tour coincided with the height of the wet season. When eventually I got home, I felt utterly exhausted and depressed and discouraged. We had had endless difficulties with the car; two nights had been spent on the roadside; the response had been poor with only very small clinics at each place; the financial outlay had been very considerable, and I felt it just was not worth it. But the real cause of my depression was simply that I could not put my heart into backing up the vision of others when I felt it ran contrary to my own. I had certainly not learnt the grace sufficient for every need, nor the joy of being spent for Him in just any way that He might direct.

Back at Nebobongo the hospital was being developed, particularly on the surgical side, and much attention was being paid to the efficient training of the nurses ('male ward orderlies' is probably a more accurate description of our lads!) in ward care and technique. I continued with the school teaching, but now I had to learn to work with others. I found I couldn't have the lads just when I wanted them; they might well be involved in a ward-round, or even in theatre. Nor could I keep them late in school as I often did in the past, for other folk had their timetables to arrange as well. In my heart, I fought against these changes. Dr Harris would invite me to carry my share of the work in the hospital and to join him in the theatre, as had been planned at the field conference, so that I could learn surgery with him before going south. God overruled and undertook for us, but there is no denying that it was a stormy year! So many times my spirit rebelled. I was quick and impulsive, where my colleague was slow and methodical. Our African fellow-workers were quick to spot the lack of cooperation and failure in agreement on many matters, and some would have played us off the one against the other.

The sense of frustration and of failure grew. The devil made accusations on every level. My free, happy, outgoing love to the Africans was turned against me in my heart as I began to feel that I loved them more than my own white fellow-workers. I loved to go and spend a weekend with Pastor Ndugu in the bush, sharing his home and meals just as though I was one of the family, and found that I enjoyed it more than being invited to another missionary's home. My heart accused me on the level of Christian living. I was so often irritable, and there were even occasions when temper flared up inside me as I felt that a faithful African fellow-worker had been misjudged or wrongly treated. My heart seemed so hard. I was so often critical and proud in my outlook. Along with this my communion with the Lord shrivelled, prayer became a formality, Bible reading a burden. I longed for liberation and peace and joy.

This sense of frustration need never have occurred had we been more willing to recognize each other's gifts. Life would have been easier if we had all realized that one approach may be needed for a pioneer work starting almost from scratch, but that other methods may be required as the work becomes established and less makeshift. Surely we all know that God has His pioneers; but He also has His consolidators. And it might have been easier for both of us if we had not tried to mix our differing gifts, but had each been given separate opportunities for their fulfilment.

Be that as it may, in my own eyes I felt again that I was a failure, empty, cold, unreal. It seemed I was putting on an act, with mixed motives, and deep in my heart, cold doubt began to rear its head. I faced again the old taunting of the devil. Are you really saved? Could you be so hard and critical, could you lose your temper, could you be so jealous of another, if the Lord Jesus was really dwelling in you? You preach it all, but you don't live it. It isn't real! With my white fellow-workers I felt keenly frustrated. The root cause was misunderstanding. I felt they were critical and had misjudged much of the work just on the reports of others without coming to see it first hand. Equally, I felt a growing barrier with my African friends, since I feared to share with them in the freedom of previous years, sensing that my somewhat unconventional approach only served to increase 'white' antagonism. And so I felt alienated almost from God Himself. There seemed to be no contact, just a sad yearning and loneliness.

One morning, I was taking morning prayers with our Nebobongo family, reading from Philippians 3:1-11. I chalked a large red cross on the blackboard, and listed on the left all the things man counted dear unto himself— public opinion, popularity, worldly wealth, security, etc. Above this I wrote the word 'dung'. To the right I placed the words, 'That I may know Him.' Suddenly the Holy Spirit came down on the congregation, and with much crying many made their way to the front and got right with God. The move started amongst the pupil midwives, but spread rapidly to the student nurses and workmen. My heart cried out to God. How could I be used in this manner to bring others to the foot of the cross, to repentance, to joy of salvation, and all the time my own heart was so cold and untouched? I turned to the African elders and blurted out the depths of my own needs. Then I rushed from the church. Back in my own home I threw myself on the ground in a desperate, frantic plea before God for His mercy and grace to be extended to myself also.

The work of God continued in the church for several hours, amidst strong tears and joyous singing. Pastor Ndugu was passing through Nebobongo on his bicycle on his way to Ibambi, and hearing the noise, went to the church to see what was happening. There the church elders told him what had occurred and described how I had left the church. He came to see me. Quietly he sat beside me and listened to my broken, somewhat incoherent outburst. Then he left and continued on his way to Ibambi. That afternoon he returned, went to see Dr Harris and then came across to see me. He had Mr Scholes's permission to take me away to his home village for a week or so. He just told me to pack a haversack and get my bicycle, and together we cycled the sixteen miles to his village. There he gave me a room in his house-and there followed seven days of prayer and fasting. At first the heavens seemed as brass, the Bible cold and meaningless. By Sunday evening, I felt I could bear no more of it. If the Lord did not meet with me I would accept that I was a castaway. I would continue my ministry to the African church as a teacher for the nurses, I would continue to teach the Word of God which I never for a moment doubted to be the absolute and certain truth, but I would not accept a missionary's allowance. I joined the Pastor and his wife round the fire, out in the verandah, as the others of the village scattered to their homes at about 10 p.m. We sat in silence, a silence you could feel, almost hear. As they earnestly prayed, slowly the Spirit of God reached through into my heart and broke down the barriers of pride, the frigid restraint, and revealed so much of self. He helped me to unburden my heart, to reveal all the rottenness and sense of failure, the fears and criticisms, the pride and selfishness. Then, so gently and quietly, Pastor Ndugu took up my words, point by point, and led me to look away from myself to the Christ of Calvary. He dealt with the need of restitution on certain points, the need of apologizing and asking forgiveness on certain others, and a great calm came.

Four amazing days followed, spent in the presence of the Lord. It is hard to describe or put on paper the preciousness of that week, spent alone, utterly given over to the influence of the Holy Spirit speaking through the pages of Holy Scripture. My mind seemed to be more crystal-clear than I had ever known. I felt no need of sleep; I had no consciousness of hunger, nor of any bodily pain or discomfort. There was a tremendous, overwhelming sense of His presence, a deep awe and wonder, I felt caught up, as it were. Even time seemed to pass with no reality. I met Him. There was little or no emotional involvement. But there was a great sense of eternal reality, of light, of truth.

I remember cycling back to Nebobongo early Monday morning to be in time for a new week in school and wondering how to share with my African friends what the Lord had done for me. When I arrived, there were three senior student nurses on the verandah. They came over to take my bicycle and haversack, and at once began praising the Lord and shaking my hand as they saw the light of happiness in my eyes! I didn't have to say anything. Then they told me that for four years, ever since 1953 when the Lord first started to pour out revival blessing on the church, they had been praying daily for me that I would let the Lord work in my heart as He had in theirs. What faithful, loving friends surrounded me.

This was not the end of the battle—by no means! It might almost be called preparation for the next round. During the next few months the devil sought every means of causing dissension and discouragement as he so often does when we seek to make a new beginning with God. On every side, I felt his attacks. I felt I was almost too tired to continue to accept the pressure of medical responsibility, and at times I felt that I would gladly have continued as a missionary if it could be without the title of doctor. I could never get away from myself or my responsibilities. Wherever I went, I was still the doctor and a crowd of patients would gather. A weekend off duty simply was not possible, and yet it was becoming very necessary after five years' steady work. I was tired of sharing my home with one and another, and the lack of privacy that this involved. And yet I felt deeply convicted by my attitude, knowing how readily others had shared their homes with me. I still felt misunderstood and criticized (possibly where nothing was intended) concerning my manner of living and eating, my friendship and unity with the Africans, my passionate desire for the setting up of the mobile village ministry, and other issues.

Added to all this, news from my dear mother and family was not happy at this time, and my heart ached to be back in England, possibly to give my mother a home, and to care for her and love her. No doubt sheer physical weariness at the end of five years of intensive work added to the struggle. I was also very hard at work trying to complete a textbook for the nurses' school in Swahili before going on furlough—typing out the manuscript, correcting proofs, preparing stencils, duplicating some hundred copies of each page, and then putting them together for our Mission press to bind.

I had eventually received permission to commence village clinics. Now that Dr Harris was also at Nebobongo to carry responsibility for the hospital and station work, I had opened forty clinics covering a four-hundred-mile circular tour. Alternate weeks I spent on the station, teaching nurses and primary school, and helping in hospital and maternity work. The weeks in between I spent out in the district visiting these forty clinics, seeing up to 2,500 patients a week, preaching the gospel, healing the sick, training catechists in the simple use of twelve medicines left in their care at each of these centres. Much though I loved this programme, as others had foreseen and warned, it was tremendously tiring and exacting and should never have been commenced at the end of one's term of service.

During the last months before furlough, Susan came into my life and home. She was a foster-child of Pastor Ndugu, a girl about sixteen years old. Owing to the fact that she had been expelled for persistently breaking school rules, she had only had about four years of primary school teaching. Following this she lived for several years with her foster-parents in the village, rebellious and hard. But at last she had responded to the claims of the Lord on her life, and came to Nebobongo to train as a midwife. But within three months, she had been found to have the dreaded marks of leprosy. It nearly broke her heart and we had a hard battle to hold on to her for the Lord. At last He won, and she agreed to come and live with me and to help in the home, whilst attending classes with the other pupils, but sitting apart. We became very close friends and I shall never forget the wonderful early morning hours, spent round the fire with cups of coffee, studying the Word and praying together. We worked together through the first three books of the Bible, preparing notes in Swahili for a future commentary for the church. At this time also I was invited again to take morning prayers on the station, and it was a great joy to study and search out, and then present, the great truths of Scripture through the Letter to the Colossians, an hour a day for three months.

Then in June 1958, my brother and his wife and son prepared to visit me, as they were travelling home to England for a year's leave after nine years in South Africa. Great preparations were made to receive them! Susan and I travelled all one night to Stanleyville to meet them at the airfield. They were unfortunately delayed, and after waiting forty-eight hours for them, I set out on the return journey the following evening. Many advised me to wait till morning, but I was impatient. I drove all night and at 5 a.m. we left the road as I fell asleep at the wheel. By God's grace we were not killed, although the van was wrecked. After several hours of shock, I was helped by kind friends who took me back home and cared for me.

That Sunday, there were farewell services at Nebobongo as I was to leave for furlough within ten days. Pastor Ndugu preached amongst others and I shall not easily forget his gentle, gracious rebuke. He preached on Haggai 1:5-6. 'Consider your ways. Ye have sown much, and bring in little; ye eat, but ye have not enough; ye drink, but ye are not filled with drink; ye clothe you, but there is none warm; and he that earneth wages earneth wages to put it into a bag with holes.' I know that he was not preaching at me, but nevertheless I felt it nearly summed up my five years in Congo, especially my ministry at Nebobongo. There had been endless hours of sowing, yet what was there to show for it? I thought of all the love and advice and godly wisdom that had surrounded me, yet how had I benefited from it? Had it not run out as money through holes in the pocket?

My brother and family came the next Monday, and we had a marvellous three or four days together, using Philip Ndugu's car to show them all round our area. Everywhere we went they were given a tremendous welcome. They left on their way home to England on the Friday morning, and the following week I also left by air for my first furlough. I had a month at home with my mother before entering the Tropical Hospital for treatment for chronic amoebic dysentery, and later for an appendectomy. I was very ill during the initial treatment. Due to this illness, and the heavy sedation I was being given, plus the great weariness after five years of missionary service, I allowed myself again to become depressed. I still had not learnt how closely linked are physical and spiritual health. This all-too-simple ruse of Satan to call reaction, failure, seemed to catch me out each time in seasons of strain and weariness.

Whilst in hospital, I received a letter from my sister Diana. She was a nun in an Anglican enclosed order, a contemplative community. She had had special permission to write to me when they heard how ill I was, and sent, under constraint of the Holy Spirit, a few verses from Hosea 2:14-16. 'Therefore, behold, I will allure her and bring her into the wilderness, and speak comfortably unto her. And I will give her her vineyards from thence, and the valley of Achor for a door of hope: and she will sing there, as in the days of her youth, and as in the day when she came up out of the land of Egypt. And it shall be at that day, saith the Lord, that thou shalt call me Ishi; and shalt call me no more Baali.' These were not verses that would normally be chosen to send to someone sick in hospital, but without doubt, they were the verses the Lord had chosen for me, to wake me from a state of lethargy, and to deliver me from this frequent accusation of the devil

about being a castaway. 'The valley of Achor for a door
of hope.' It was a great promise looking forward to future
triumph. In the valley of Achor Joshua had dealt drastically
with Achan's sin, the disobedience which had brought defeat
on the children of Israel as they pressed forward into Canaan
following the victory at Jericho. The cause of their defeat was
put out of the camp and faith in God for future victory was
restored. So God's judgments become the gateway through
which we enter into His promises and go on to possess our
own inheritance in Him.

Immediately following my five weeks in hospital,
I embarked on a series of deputation meetings covering
a large area of the British Isles. It lasted for twelve packed
weeks, and I loved every moment of it! We were so busy
I had not time for introspection! I was extremely nervous
at every meeting, and felt a great burden to find the Lord's
mind and message each day. But He blessed abundantly.
I spoke mainly about the Revival, but often told also my
own testimony, how hardness of heart and pride had held me
back from entering into the full blessing for four long years,
but how eventually, through the ministry of Africans, He
broke my pride and dealt with me also. Many people were
challenged during those weeks of meetings, and several
testified that their lives had been completely changed as they
met anew with the Lord. I was wonderfully happy; but once
again, my personality being what it was, I found success and
popularity going to my head. All the time I had to watch
and pray that my rejoicing should be only in Him.

The following Christmas, at a Graduates' Fellowship
Conference at Swanwick, through the prayerful interest of
a doctor friend, I was put in touch with the Mildmay Mission
Hospital in Bethnal Green, East London, and in February
started there as a Houseman and Casualty Officer. It was
strange being back in an English hospital, and not a little
terrifying. Almost immediately, we were in the throes of
an influenza epidemic. All hospital beds were taken over
for the acute chest cases and many elderly people died. We
seemed to be on duty almost twenty-four hours at a stretch,
and I found I was working longer and more tiring hours

even than in Congo! Time for quiet and prayer in the early morning was almost non-existent. I was often too tired, and fell asleep when I tried to pray. How common an experience amongst Christian Housemen! It is well for us to remember that God understands and that a quiet time of a particular length and pattern is not a kind of magic formula, the one essential mark of the keen Christian. Rather, it is the spiritual attitude of heart and mind that counts and sustains at such periods. I loved the work, and threw myself wholeheartedly into every part of it, including ward services and prayers for the out-patients down in Casualty. I made every effort to be absolutely conscientious in my work for each of the different consultants who visited the hospital and was pleased when they seemed satisfied. Once again, I was driven forward by the desire to be a success.

This was a time when I began to look back and to compare the work I was doing at Mildmay with that in the Congo. Also I began to receive a monthly cheque for the very first time in my life! This brought a sense of security. I could buy things for my mother and her home; I could plan for us to go on holiday together. I was also putting aside for my return to the Congo, and sending monthly gifts to help them at Nebobongo. But the work at Nebobongo and its importance began to change colour, so to speak. I recalled the things that had occurred out there, the criticisms that had been made, the failures in relationships, the many frustrations in the work. Previously, I had been willing for the Lord to show me that I was at fault. I wanted Him to deal with me, to empty me of myself in order that He might mould me into the likeness of Jesus and fill me with Himself. Now it no longer seemed like that. Why was I always in the wrong? Why did I always have to give in over everything that occurred? Why hadn't the Mission put money at my disposal for the medical work? Why hadn't the menfolk at other stations been more willing to help me at Nebobongo with buildings and repairs, with sanitation and feeding problems, with the upkeep of the car and the oversight of workmen? Why in fact had they put upon me, a woman doctor, jobs which ought to be done by men? And so the devil worked his subtle business and seeds of bitterness, jealousy and envy were sown. And with it all came a growing sense of insecurity for the future and a realization of great loneliness.

Suddenly I saw the answer clearly, and apparently the way to claim the answer. With this new sense of urgency, I argued myself into believing that God owed it to me to work it all out my way. I too had the right to marry, to have a husband, someone I could lean on, someone to care for me, to protect me, to be always there as friend and counsellor, to take the responsibility, even to repair the broken furniture! Surely He could not ask me to go back again to Congo single. Perhaps for the first term of service it had been reasonable to expect this of me. There had been jobs to do that perhaps I should not have been so free for had I been married. But now, surely, it was different.

Temptation followed temptation. The devil put the thoughts and desires and growing hunger first. Then along came someone apparently eminently suited (so I thought!). Though he was a true Christian, I soon found out that he had no call to overseas missionary service. So I sought to be released from the Mission, feeling that he would never ask me to marry him whilst he knew I was committed to returning to the Congo. How subtle the adversary is! This new attack began as a desire to have someone by me in Congo. But if this was not possible, Congo would now have to be sacrificed, that I might have him for myself. We were thrown into each other's company for six long months, and I passionately desired that the Lord would give me the fulfilment of all I longed for. We had prayer and Bible reading together of an evening. We went out to services or to open-air testimony together on Sundays. He was always kindly and gracious. He never encouraged me; I only wished he would! I cut myself off from the Mission at this time, sensing that they would disapprove and knowing all the arguments they could use too well! I bought new clothes, and had my hair permed, and set myself to win him.

# 9

# Fresh Vision and Triumph

My somewhat obvious un-spiritual state at this time led many to pray for me. Some of my friends persuaded me to go away for a long weekend to Herne Bay Court. Arriving on Friday evening, tired and depressed, I went to the final meeting of the previous house-party, with little heart or interest. As my eyes were already closing, heavy with sleep, from weeks of over-tension and mental unrest, the preacher announced as his text Hosea 2:14-16, '... the valley of Achor for a door of hope.'

I do not know what he said; I do not know who he was. I only know that every nerve felt raw and alive. These were the verses my sister had sent me nine months earlier when I had been ill in hospital. I went to my room that evening, fearful, afraid to meet God, knowing what He wanted to say to me, but no longer wanting to listen. I wanted things my way now. I didn't want to be made hungry again after God; I didn't want His promise of love and comfort. I felt I had been following a will-o'-the-wisp for long enough, and I was a failure. This kind of life wasn't for me, and I didn't want to be cajoled into trying again.

I could not silence His love. The Hounds of Heaven were bearing down on me. I longed for Him with one breath. I longed for husband and home and the comfort and security this would offer with the next. I struggled till tears— burning, gasping tears—ran down my face. I struggled till exhausted. I fell asleep—He was there! I forced myself awake; I even leapt out of bed and splashed my face with cold water. I threw the window open. A gentle May breeze in the still moonlight calmed me. I slept again, and again He was there, gentle, loving, stern, demanding, beautiful, worthy. The sense of His presence faded as I sank into deep, troubled sleep. Morning light only brought back a bitter sense of battle. Why should He ask me to relinquish this that I most wanted?

I went back to London on Monday, knowing He would win—indeed had won—but nevertheless not wanting to give in, not wanting His victory, yet terrified to lose Him or to drive Him away. What a mess! How clever the devil is! I did all I could to close my ears, to refuse to listen. At the same time, I longed for deliverance, for a deliverance which the next moment I didn't want! How contrary can we be?

One morning, several weeks later, I was struck in my morning reading by Galatians 1:15, 'When it pleased God… to reveal his Son in me….' I couldn't shake off the thought. 'Can't you see? Can't you see?' a voice seemed to whisper to me. 'Christ dwells in you. It is Him you are bent on destroying, not yourself. He is you. Christ in you, the hope of glory.' I felt baffled, uncertain, unable to bear the revelation, yet this was the truth I had searched for all these years. The simple naked fact of truth—His Son in me. Not just for me, but in me.

Next week I went to Keswick. Others had made this possible for me, arranged a locum and booked for me to stay in the IVF women's camp. The one from whom I so passionately desired human security and love and strength went too. I went to almost all the meetings. I had determined that the Lord should speak to me, that I would hear and that I would obey whatever the cost. And then I left Him to do it. I can remember the tormenting thought that perhaps I had gone too far. Yet however much I had rebelled and kicked, He knew that I loved Him, that I was bound to Him for ever and longed deep down to serve Him. In my extremity, I had no-one else to whom I could turn. O God, don't leave me, don't cast me off!

On Tuesday evening I attended the meeting in the large tent, physically exhausted after having climbed painfully to the top of Scafell Pike during the day. The address was based on 2 Kings 2:1-11. Elisha's journey with Elijah, and the speaker applied it to our life's journey in retrospect. They began at Gilgal, the place of original committal (do you remember meeting Me on that evening of New Year's Day, 1945?). They passed through Bethel, the place of Jacob's vision where he erected his altar of surrender (do you remember meeting Me in the hospital that day in March 1950?), and came to Jericho, the scene of Joshua's initial victory (do you remember that day in October 1955 when I took you from Ibambi to Nebobongo?). Then Elijah offers young Elisha again the opportunity of remaining with the school of the sons of the prophets. 'Tarry here; you do not need to go any further.' But he refuses to leave Elijah. 'And they two went on' down to Jordan, down into the place of death, the place of separation from self and self-interest.

I was wide awake now, urgently listening, desperate to go on with the Lord even though it meant death to self. 'Ask what I shall do for thee', Elijah tells Elisha. And the quiet voice of the Master seemed to echo the question in my own heart.

I stayed to the after-meeting, awed, fearful, yet knowing that I must answer that voice and receive again from Him the reply. A quiet, unobtrusive counsellor came and sat by me. At last, in tears, I asked the fearful question. Could He forgive deliberate, wilful sin? Could He restore and recommission one who had chosen her own way, and I a missionary on furlough? The whole rotten story of the last few months was at last out, and with joy I knew that He had forgiven me. I told the Lord I was willing for anything He would say to me, and to do anything He asked of me, unconditionally.

I think I knew at once that I was forgiven, but I could not feel that He could 'lightly' forget. I was not sure that He would re-commission, or that He would be willing to use me further in His service. I felt that I had entered a 'second-best' experience, but my fight was over. I felt very exhausted but deeply relieved to know that He was again in charge.

The next evening, after an amazing address on temptation, my friend and I went out together and agreed to give up meeting one another. There was a deep wound in my heart, but it was the only way for any future peace. The following day, while I was still at Keswick, I received a telegram, calling me to Newport for an interview at the St Woolos Hospital in connection with a House-surgeon's job there for which I had applied. I had a deep inner conviction that God was definitely at the helm.

As the wound slowly began to heal I realized that a new calm had taken possession. The intenseness of life, the acute awareness of every situation, the passionate longings and yearnings all seemed to have been replaced by a quiet acceptance. There was a sense of resignation, perhaps; a consciousness that I had no rights—no right to quote terms, no right to expect grace, no right even to feel, to feel saved, or happy, or at peace. I accepted utterly that, by the immense immeasurable grace of God and according to His predetermined counsel, Christ was in me and that He should now live out His life and purpose as He saw fit.

I wrote at once to Mission Headquarters, thanking them for having granted me a year's leave of absence, thanking them for their sympathetic prayers during recent months, and asking them to consider my reapplication for full membership at the next quarterly staff meeting, and also to consider an application to return to the Congo in May 1960.

My six months at Mildmay having ended, I went at once to Newport and took up my duties as House-surgeon. There was no applicant for the post of Houseman to the obstetrical unit, so I helped out there as well, and had three weeks' invaluable experience, including doing my first Caesarian operation under supervision! Then the Lord arranged another opportunity for me. The boilers in the theatre sterilizing unit had to be repaired and the theatres were to be closed for three weeks. During this time, the surgical staff were going to take their annual holiday. This included the medical superintendent who was also in charge of the obstetrical unit. I was invited by the board to help out for that three weeks as an acting registrar. So I had the opportunity to learn something of the running and administration of a large British hospital, and of work in all the departments, which was to be directly related to the tasks that lay ahead, especially those of training African personnel in administration in the future Independent Congo.

The months at Newport were tremendously happy and busy ones. We worked closely as a team with ward and theatre sisters and nurses, and had plenty of night emergency calls. I had the joy of spending Christmas at hospital, and what a day it was! Dinner on the ward with staff and patients was almost a seven-course meal! We visited and chatted with everybody. The theatre staff, knowing my connection with Congo, had decorated the long corridor as a jungle track with palm fronds and elephants as a welcome to their jungle doctor! The ward service, for me the crowning joy of the day, seemed to be greatly appreciated by patients, relatives and staff alike. At the end of the service, Sister presented me with a cheque for £50 from both patients and staff to buy a general anaesthetic machine for the Nebobongo hospital. I was deeply moved by this symbol of their deep love and affection.

After Christmas we put on our 'variety show'. Hardly perhaps, the kind of task one would associate with a missionary on furlough, but strangely successful, and viewed as yet another avenue for showing the relevance of the Christian gospel to our everyday life. Each ward, each department, all the different groups of staff, including carpenters and electricians, took part, each saying thank you to the others for their part as a team in making the wheels of the hospital run smoothly. Even the Consultants joined in the grand finale which represented the crowning of the chief bard of the year at the Eisteddfod! It was a great (if amateurish) success to crown weeks of tireless preparation.

There followed three months of holiday and various meetings, including a happy week amongst the students at the Missionary Training College at Glasgow, and two weeks with friends in Northern Ireland. At the WEC quarterly staff meeting, my request to be re-admitted as a member was granted and immediately an application was made for reservations on the Castle Line ship sailing on 20th May from London to Mombasa. This was followed by the usual bustle of shopping, listing, packing, labelling, visits to shipping agents and photographers, visas and permits, and at last we were ready to go.

It was not so easy leaving mother and home this second time, especially as rumours were beginning to circulate of anticipated trouble at the declaration of Congo's Independence in just about six weeks' time. I remember my last Sunday evening at Christ Church, Bromley, when I gave a short testimony and asked their prayers for the coming term of service. 'Is anything too hard for the Lord?' Even the unrest, political upheaval, communist infiltration and influence? It might be that our days would be short; it could be that our work would be taken from us. Suffering and persecution possibly awaited us in the Congolese church. But with their prayers we could steadfastly answer, 'There is nothing too hard for Thee.'

With me on the journey out was Elaine de Rusett, an Australian nurse coming to join me at Nebobongo, and young Bill McChesney, a 24-year-old American. I remembered so clearly my first voyage and the goodness of the senior missionaries to me in fellowship and in language study. I therefore felt a great responsibility not to fail the two new recruits who were with me. Each morning, after breakfast, we met together in our two-berth cabin, for prayer and Bible study. We read together through the book of Nehemiah, and day by day I talked to them about one of the stations of the Congo field, introducing them to the workers and the background development, the present work and situation and needs, and as far as I could, the Africans at each place. During each day I encouraged them to give some time to language study and helped them all I could. One day on board, after I had apparently been 'mothering' them, a dear elderly lady came up to me and asked if Bill and Elaine were my two delightful children? That cured me, much to their delight! I myself benefited considerably, of course, from going steadily through the Swahili again and revising my knowledge of both grammar and vocabulary. In the afternoon, I had the joy of helping another group of friends on the boat with their Swahili language study. They were going to Kenya in Government service. There was plenty of time for quiet, for prayer and study, for meditation, for letter-writing, and reading books.

At Genoa we had three days in the port whilst cargo was being loaded. We wandered over the town together. I can still see clearly a great storage shed down by the docks with a huge notice in Italian forbidding trespassers. Bill sauntered up to the door with his usual charming, disarming smile, and wandered in to look round. I was horrified and pleaded with him to come out. The last thing I wanted was to run into trouble in a foreign land where we were not known and did not know the language. Bill looked at my troubled face and grinned impishly. 'What's up? "The world belongs to all of us, so make yourself at home".' 'Bill,' I said, 'Can't you read the notice?' 'No; me no read Italiano.' What a lad! Always full of fun, yet always so gracious and courteous. We walked the whole circle of the town, along the hilltops, following the ruined fortifications and walls, collecting wild flowers which he would send to his mother. She was not to see him again. Just over four years later, he was martyred at Wamba during the Simba rebellion.

On arrival at Mombasa we were forcibly reminded of the difficult days that lay ahead. The day previously, while still at sea, I had received a cablegram asking me to consider seriously the advisability of staying in Nairobi until after the Declaration of Independence in Congo, so that we could see how things would go. The sender, a relative of one of our missionaries, pleaded with me to think twice before taking these two new recruits into such obvious danger. At Mombasa the customs officials and immigration officers would not stamp our passports nor give us leave to get off the ship, until we had pledged our return fares to England. They told us that, with still a fortnight to go before the Declaration of Independence, white refugees were already pouring into Kenya and Uganda from Congo. They advised us strongly to continue the round journey and to go home!

They pointed out forcibly that they could not accommodate all these refugees in their countries, and therefore could not take the deliberate responsibility of adding three more to their problems. We pledged our return fares and left the ship. As we went down the gangway, carrying suitcases and briefcases, an African porter came straight up to Bill, the only man in our group, and took his baggage, leaving us women to struggle with ours. Bill laughed, and felt he had at last reached a country that did things the right way round! Then he reached out and gave us a hand.

The shipping agent, Mrs Passmore, had us cleared through customs in no time, and everything was soon on to the train. So began our long journey up country through Kenya and Uganda. I was wise to some of the problems this time, especially in regard to the necessity of ordering a 'night-sack' with blankets from the guard. On my first journey no-one had told me how bitterly cold it could feel after sunset, as we climbed 5,000 feet up to Nairobi away from the stifling heat of sea-level, and I had frozen all night! At Kikuyu station, as the train shunted to a stop, there was my college friend, Sylvia, with a vast dog, come to meet us! It was quite exciting to meet up in the middle of Africa for just a ten-minute chat on a railway platform. She was teaching then at the Kikuyu Girls' High School.

On again, to Kampala, where we had to 'fill in time' for several hours, waiting for our connection to take us on to the head of the railroad. This final stretch of the journey took us through the most glorious mountainous country, up and up towards the Congo-Uganda border. I felt heavy with the responsibility of taking these two with me towards the dangers that everyone threatened, although of course both of them had made their own decisions before the Lord. But I was earnestly hoping that one of the senior missionaries would meet us at Kasese and, having read the cablegram I had received on the ship, make the actual final decision. What a joy as we piled out of the train, to see Frank Cripps waiting with the Mission truck! In no time we were loaded up, and piled in, Elaine and Bill travelling with Frank Bates, a young Australian missionary who had also come to meet us, and myself with Frank Cripps whose special responsibility was the Mission press and the training of Congolese printers. Soon we were over the border and through customs without the slightest difficulty. A little further on a halt was called at the roadside to sing the doxology and to thank God for having safely brought us thus far, into the promised land, surely 'for such a time as this' (Esther 4:14).

# 10

# Treasures of Darkness

What a welcome home! Did one ever fear that perhaps one wasn't really wanted? All along the route in, as we passed each out-church and village clearing where I had worked and preached, we were greeted by crowds of school children, together with the evangelist, catechist and their wives, all waving and cheering. Then at Ibambi, what joy it was to see again the Bible school students, printshop workers, school children, nurses, all singing and happy and shaking hands. Finally, we reached Nebobongo itself to be met with big hugs and kisses of welcome home, and their 'special' hymn, 'Stand up, stand up, for Jesus, ye soldiers of the cross', learnt for the occasion. It was a thrilling day indeed—walking all round the station with John and Elsie Harris and their two small children, David and Lois, to see all the improvements and new buildings and permanent roofs, and then down to the village to greet all our dear Africans and fellow-workers.

John and Elsie were very tired. They had been out seven years, hard years with many changes involving two different language areas, and they had both had spells of sickness. They were ready for furlough and glad to hand over the responsibility. So I was back into harness once more, and how good it felt! There was need to walk carefully, to 'feel' the new climate of opinion with Independence only two weeks away. I listened in to all I could, nurses, patients, village men from over the way, and also radio reports from

Stanleyville and Leopoldville. There were rumours, stories, vague threats, unrest and uncertainty.

One evening that week there was a meeting of our station elders and the male nurses in the dispensary. After a while they sent for us whites, all four of us. They were polite, but were obviously leading up to something. Eventually Joseph Bumukumu brought it out. 'We want to appoint an African leader', he said. 'Everywhere else has done it. At the Red Cross Hospital Dr Kadoner has handed over authority to a senior male orderly, Gwo-gwo, and he has become the new director. We want you to hand over to John Mangadima.' We waited, tense, a little uncertain, praying hard for wisdom. Then John Mangadima himself spoke, and saved a difficult situation. 'I don't mind being in charge of the nurses and the general administrative work. But I'm not a doctor and we can't do without our doctors, and I couldn't ever be over them.' All round there was a gentle 'letting-out' of held breath. They were content; we had not refused their request, but they themselves had made their choice that they wanted us to stay. We were quite clear that there was to be a new emphasis of authority, but we were equally sure that He would steer us through the initial rapids.

So 30th June came. For us it was a day of prayer and praise, with a football match in the afternoon, and a sense of waiting. Mayaribu, the headman of the nearest village, came to visit us, with six other senior village men from the immediate vicinity. They came wearing colourful, native straw hats and flowers, each carrying a little bouquet of flowers and some eggs. We went out on to the verandah to greet them, and Mayaribu made a little speech of welcome saying that they, the headmen of the region, invited us, their 'strangers', to stay with them in their new Independence. We were thus publicly 'accepted'. It was a moving moment, and we responded accordingly.

In the following days, all work continued as usual in the hospital and maternity compound, the only difference being the oft-heard cry 'Uhuru!'—Freedom! Liberty! Everyone seemed to be carrying a bouquet of flowers and wearing native hats and loin-cloths like their forefathers in place of the European clothing which was more usual in our area. Slowly the initial fear and tension relaxed, and somewhat amazedly, we accepted that Independence had come without demonstration or lawlessness.

Suddenly a different note was sounded. There was mutiny in the army at Leopoldville, which led to the rapid evacuation of Belgians and their families following wickedness and the raping of white women. Panic filled the air. Overnight, the whole picture changed. On Thursday, 15th July, two Mission cars passed our station going north. Later in the afternoon they returned with others, and called us all to go to a meeting that evening at Ibambi. Two of our senior missionaries had arrived that day at Nebobongo for medical care. Together the six of us, soberly and wondering, made our way to the centre. We began to gather in, until eventually there must have been over twenty of us. Everyone had different stories to tell, things seen, things heard, things feared. It was very hard to think levelly in such an atmosphere of anxiety. Truckloads of soldiers had gone through that very day, singing in local tribal languages of what they would do to us on their return. Within an hour, some fifteen of the missionaries had signed a list to say they wanted to go over the border, at least temporarily, to see whether things would settle down. Soon the great evacuation had begun. Throughout the night they packed and sorted and left, car after car. So it was that next day, tired and puzzled, I found myself back at Nebobongo alone. Alone, that is, so far as white companionship was concerned. It was a strange feeling. Even my car had gone to help carry those who felt they should leave. And yet there was a quiet peace, knowing that He had brought me to Congo for such a time as this. We tidied up the two missionaries' houses, packing away everything as neatly as possible, and then had a meeting in the church to discuss our immediate future. I found I was surrounded by a love and sense of security and protection that I had never known before. A deep new bond had been forged, and I knew that it was indeed He who had told me to stay with them at this moment of their great need.

Together we decided that the church elders should be formed into an executive committee responsible for all station affairs, spiritual and material. Agoya was appointed President, Mangadima as secretary, and Basuana was made responsible for the youth. The three together were to act as treasurer. I was unanimously asked to remain with them as advisor and friend in all matters. We had a wonderful time of prayer and praise.

That evening, a truck full of soldiers passed. During the night, alone in that large house, each time a rat scurried over the bamboo ceilings I started up in fear. At about 2 a.m. I got up, and knelt in prayer, and asked the Lord to liberate me from this dreadful fearfulness, and if He would, to send me someone to sleep in the house with me. I hadn't even got back into bed when there was a knock at the back door. I was terrified! This was it! They'd come for me. I could hardly force myself to ask who was there. 'We are', they answered, 'Mama Taadi and Mama Damaris.' I flung the door open, and burst into tears as I drew them into the house. The Lord woke us from sleep (in different houses, on opposite sides of the compound) and told us to come and sleep in your house so that you wouldn't be alone in these dangerous days.' I hugged them, made them up a couple of beds, made us each a cup of Ovaltine; we read Daily Light together and then settled down again for the rest of the night.

Next day the Lord sent two other white ladies to join me, missionaries from another WEC station forty miles to the north. It was agreed that we should stay together for the first period of Independence until we saw how things would be. It was a joy to welcome them. I remember that first evening discussing at prayers together the recent puzzling events leading up to the evacuation of half the Mission and the fact that the final straw had been the threat of rape to white women by the mutineering army. Surely the Lord had died on Calvary for this as much as any other sin? It wasn't our sin or shame. We could remain pure before the Lord with His purity no matter what happened. Fifty years ago missionaries risked their lives from malaria or wild animals. Today it might be a different price they had to pay, a different danger to face; but surely He was still the same wonderful Lord who was worthy of any sacrifice made?

We had a month together, dividing up the work and responsibilities between us and doing everything alongside the Africans, helping them daily to carry more and more, of the responsibilities. Many times they would say, 'What shall we do if you also have to leave us?' One weekend soldiers did visit us. I was away at Pastor Ndugu's village at the time. They made no trouble. We heard of troubles in other areas; rumours in fact abounded. But we saw little or nothing to trouble us. We often went up to Ibambi to discuss plans with the missionaries there. On one of these visits we heard of the decision which was eventually taken for two of our menfolk to go to the Ugandan border to collect those who had evacuated, those, that is, that now wanted to return. So on Friday, 20th August 1960, just four weeks from their departure, we prepared a huge meal for seventeen at Nebobongo, to welcome them home again. As they drove in we ran out to greet them looking especially for our nurse, whom we were so anxious to have come back to help us in the maternity compound, the hospital, and the leprosy camp. What a deep blow of disappointment it was to find there was no nurse in the party for Nebobongo! Yet here too, doubtless, the Lord was working, as it forced my hand to put more and more responsibility on the African nurses and midwives.

Elaine de Ruseti joined me for two happy weeks, to glean all she could of Congolese dispensary ways and tropical drugs and dosages before going 250 miles northwest to our furthermost station to help them. Then again I had four weeks alone, my two lady friends having returned to their own station. This was a very busy period indeed, a foretaste of what lay ahead. In our immediate area of 200 miles radius, where there had previously been seventeen doctors and surgeons, we were now reduced to three, one a leprologist, one a pathologist and myself. We were faced with the difficulty of emergency surgery, none of us being trained or practised in such. Patients came to us from terrific distances, some having been carried through the forest for several days slung in a blanket on a pole between the shoulders of two carriers, and their condition on arrival was often too awful for description. Sometimes we worked round the clock. Weariness became habitual. To hear a truck drive up ceased to cause the fearful dread of soldiers but brought instead an equal horror as to what new emergency was being brought in. God enabled me through those weeks, even though a severe mental battle raged, to learn to trust Him for each needed victory.

Trouble was reported a hundred miles south. As a result three missionaries were brought north and came to live at Nebobongo-one of them being Florence Stebbing, with whom I had worked for the previous five years! She took over at once the oversight of the maternity work and leprosarium, but there, too, she had many difficulties. Since Independence an African midwife, Naomi, had been placed in charge. She was apparently doing very well, and appeared to be teachable. But she did not like having to work alongside a European again, and created much unpleasantness for Miss Stebbing. They were certainly not easy days. We longed to help our African colleagues, and to trust them, and to give them the authority they coveted. Yet we had to see to the maintenance of medical discipline—hygiene, cleanliness, locking up and signing for dangerous drugs—all of which they were beginning to think were merely 'white obsessions'.

An urgent call came from the young Congolese Government that I would go to help them at the hospital at Wamba, sixty miles east across the Nepoko river. So I started to work two days a week at Wamba, doing ward-rounds and operations and clinics for Africans and Europeans. It involved leaving home at 5.30 a.m. to be at the hospital by 8 a.m. Sometimes we did not finish until after 8 o'clock at night which meant not getting home until 10.30 p.m. Weariness increased. The work was not satisfying at Wamba, as I had no authority over the nursing staff and knew full well that the treatment I ordered was frequently not given. Discipline was almost unknown amongst them, and certainly none had the slightest understanding of a professional conscience towards the patients and towards the accurate administration of drugs.

On Tuesday, 13th February 1961, I set off for Wamba as usual, accompanied by John Mangadima, who was going to assist me at the day's operative list. Six miles from Wamba we were flagged to a halt at one of the out churches, and warned to return. 'There is great trouble in Wamba. All the whites are being tied up. Go home.' We argued that as medicals this was not possible. We had a responsibility to our patients. Whilst we discussed the matter, the crowd of casual passengers that had been travelling to Wamba by my van disappeared with all their goods! Mangadima and I continued alone. I had urged him also to remain and wait for me at the church. 'Never', he exclaimed. 'If it is safe for you to go, I go with you.' Just before Wamba we were stopped by wild rough soldiers at a barrier. Menacingly they commanded me out of the car. John stopped their wicked intentions by saying, 'Do not touch her! She is "one of us", our doctor', using a word in the local tongue meaning 'blood of our blood'; and they desisted. They took us into town to the Government offices. Here, as their doctor, I was promptly promised free passage, despite the curfew imposed on all other Europeans. Even as they spoke, two Belgian planters were brought in and roughly thrown into an inner courtyard. Fearfully, we went on to the hospital, where we heard the reason for it all. That morning, the report of the murder of Patrice Lumumba had arrived. Not a single nurse had remained at the hospital and there was nothing we could do. We went to our Mission station a quarter of a mile from the Government post where there were four missionaries working, and discussed with them the present dangerous situation. Then we set out to return home. At the large junction of three roads six miles out there were barriers across all the roads and numerous soldiers were inspecting the cars and trucks lined up on all sides, searching for hidden Europeans. We pulled in, turned off the engine, and settled down for a long wait. Suddenly, we were waved forward. We drew out, and as we approached, the barriers were taken down, each soldier came to attention and smartly saluted us. We sailed through! God had gone before us and caused someone among the soldiers to recognize my car. Presumably they had received instructions from the Wamba Government to treat 'their doctor' with respect.

It was not always so easy. Two of our senior lady missionaries working in the southern area of our Province were grievously ill-treated and humiliated by the women's group of the Lumumba party. These women were quite as wicked and ferocious as the most brutal of the soldiers. Miss Kingdon at Wamba was threatened many times. I was stopped one day in Wamba High Street, as I set out home after a day of operating, because one of my indicator lights had not worked. Forced from the car at gun-point and driven into the police courtroom, I was held there at attention for over two hours.

We never knew what they might do next. One night about this time, thieves broke into my house. Apparently they had drugged (or attempted to poison) me. But my dog had eaten most of my supper as I was not hungry, and she died next day. They stripped the house of curtains, cloths, jumpers, cutlery, foodstuffs, even my glasses and watch from the very room where I was asleep in bed. It left a horrid fear for weeks, making sleep very difficult.

Heart-break followed. One Sunday evening, Miss Stebbing and I were having prayers together. We heard a noise from the maternity compound and listened intently. Was this the noise of the outpoured Holy Spirit, of revival blessing? Yet something did not ring true in our hearts, and with a lantern we set out to investigate. We met Mama Taadi and Mama Damaris coming up from the village, also attracted by the noise and with the same thoughts in their hearts. Together we walked across. We found our four senior midwives and several pupils, dressed in their native clothes instead of hospital uniform, having a meeting in the compound, singing and beating an empty forty-gallon drum, and dancing. Before I had time to investigate further, Mama Taadi called me aside and asked the two of us to go back home. We did and prayed earnestly for wisdom and guidance.

Two hours later, the two Bible women joined us and told us the sad story. The crowd, with the midwives, had been singing in the native tongue songs of filth and mockery, to our hymn tunes, deliberately imitating many of the expressions of the times of the revival. They were joking about and jeering at God and all that is holy to us. In the wards, in the midwives' homes, in various parts of their compound, more than ten men from surrounding villages were surprised, and sent off. We spent the night in prayer, our hearts heavy with grief, a deep sense of failure and disappointment mingled with righteous indignation and horror at the wickedness that had been deliberately perpetrated by those whom we trusted, those in charge, those who had been preaching the gospel in the wards and clinics each day.

We spent the next day in prayer and fasting, and sent out into the area for the parents of all the midwives and pupils, and for the Church Council for the area. On Tuesday we all met together, and eventually it was unanimously decided that the maternity compound must be closed and all the girls dismissed. We must make a fresh start. The girls appeared to be amused, certainly in no wise subdued nor troubled. They went off, laughing and joking. Was it bravado? Was it a cloak, a bluff? How we longed that this might be so. Every girl was told clearly in the hearing of her parents, that if she was repentant and attended regularly at her local church, we would consider her readmission to the training school the following September term. They left; and within five months we heard that more than half of them were expecting babies. I thought my heart would break. How had I failed them? Where had we gone wrong? 'Independence' meant only this to so many, the removal of all restraints, throwing over all discipline, living as they liked, as unto themselves.

That same evening, as I drove to Wamba to take two pupils back to their parents, I arrived at the Mission station there just in time to assist at one of our missionaries' confinements, her first little one, a lovely girl! It certainly was a precious end to a tragic day, though it served to highlight the cunning of the devil in taking one of God's most precious gifts and debasing it into lust.

By this time, we were beginning to know many shortages. Village shops had none of the essentials that we wanted, powdered milk, salt, matches, sugar, flour. Even petrol and paraffin were very hard to get. Many Europeans had taken their cars off the road. For six weeks we had had no letters from home, which also meant no allowances. We did not know what it all meant, except that our Province was being boycotted by the rest of the Congo to make us toe the line. I was one of the very few still travelling to and fro, and therefore became the postman for our own local mail, calling in at all the plantations and shops and the Roman Catholic compounds on my way to and from Wamba. We had a good Administrator, and his assistant was also very friendly and kindly to us. One day I took all our Intermediate Campaigner Clan, boys and girls, about twenty-four of them, all in uniform and carrying flags, to greet the Administrator at the Wamba territorial headquarters. As we arrived, we found that it was an important public occasion, with a party political harangue from one of the Ministers up from Stanleyville. My young folk stood at ease, in ranks, by the central flagstaff, in full sunshine, for two hours, listening to an impassioned political speech in a language that hardly any of us could understand! Making our way forward afterwards, I was led up the steps to be introduced to the Minister as 'their doctor', and in turn I was able to introduce the youngsters. They sang to him, and saluted, and drilled. Then he gave a further twenty minutes' speech on their behalf! He spoke very highly of them, and stressed the need of putting God first if Congo was to advance, and the need for all young people to learn discipline and obedience and hard work if they wanted to help their country forward. It was a great day!

The first anniversary of Independence Day was approaching. Schools had to be closed beforehand, as many people feared an outbreak of trouble. The church planned a day of conference for prayer and praise at Ibambi. Our Campaigner Clans at Nebobongo set off at 5.30 a.m. to march the seven miles to Ibambi, before the sun got too hot. There were about ninety of us, all in uniform and with flags flying, singing every step of the way—for those who could keep enough breath going! The church was well packed with over 2,500 of our local Christians attending. During the day, I did not feel too well, and by evening, when it was time to set off on the march home, I was very glad indeed to be offered a lift in a car. On Saturday we had a sports day arranged by the Boy Campaigners to which they had invited young men from the local plantations and the fat factory, and also the regional chieftain. It was a very hot and tiring day, which I thought accounted for my headache and feeling of fever. By Sunday, I realized that I was not well, but managed to struggle through the day's services, including the wonderful Communion Service in the evening when four of the Europeans from Ibambi joined us. On Monday I stayed in bed, and that was the beginning of a long illness.

Through that first week I remained at Nebobongo. Suzanne and Elena, two African nurses, slept in the home with me and did all they could to look after me. I tried to help with seeing hospital charts daily and giving any advice I could but the fever stayed high, and interludes of delirium and great depression alternated. Treatment seemed to be ineffective. The following week I was moved to Ibambi, to relieve Elaine and Florence, who already had all they could manage. At Ibambi I was nursed by Miss Muriel Harman. I suffered another week of swinging temperatures and ever-increasing weakness, constant vomiting and severe headaches, before eventually the illness began to respond to treatment, and at last, after five weeks, the fever ended. I was very thin and appallingly weak. Just as I began to get up and sit in a chair, I developed jaundice and seemed to be as ill again as the previous week. This dragged on for another ten days. I felt embarrassed at being a burden to everyone, and so on 13th August I asked to be allowed to go back to Nebobongo, and slowly to resume my work. The two missionaries there had had a heavy time during those six weeks. However, the weakness just dogged me and made me virtually unable to do anything. Ten days later, I felt I could go on no longer, I was just too weak to do anything. I vomited everything I tried to eat; the pain never let up. I felt the end was very near, and asked my two co-workers to call the church elders.

Even as I asked, they arrived at the back-door saying that the Lord had constrained them to come to anoint me in the name of the Lord. They prayed for me, anointing me and believing for His touch of healing. To me it was an act of obedience according to James 5:14, but I did not ask for healing. In a few hours the vomiting ceased, the pain eased, and I fell into a restful sleep. Next day, others had arranged for me to go away to Egbita, to the two lady friends who had stayed with me at Nebobongo the previous year, and a car came to collect me and take me to them. There was still an overwhelming weariness and weakness, but certainly less pain. And from that day, I slowly recovered. I spent six wonderful weeks at Egbita, being utterly spoilt and nursed back to health. Towards the end of my stay I spent hours each day preparing lecture notes in French for the coming school year for the nurses. It was very moving to realize how much the believing prayers of our Africans had played in my recovery, how they were growing towards maturity and making decisions for us, instead of our always making them for them.

When I got home for the next school year, early in October, my work at the Government hospital at Wamba had finished, for they now had regular visits from a UNO doctor. There were five doctors in the area, two of them excellent surgeons, and the terrible strains began to let up. But the shortages increased, and what goods there were we could purchase only at black-market prices. Blankets that I used to buy for the patients at 17s 6d were now over £3. Bowls and buckets could not be obtained. Penicillin was unheard of. We were down to our last thermometer. So in May 1952, I went the long 250-mile journey to Stanleyville with two Africans to see what we could do. We visited the Labour Exchange to discuss the possibility of getting permission for the local chiefs' men to build us new wards at the chiefs' expense. We visited the Treasury to discuss the possibility of the nurses receiving Government salaries. We visited the hospital and the Minister of Health to discuss our need of drugs and equipment. We visited UNO Headquarters and discussed everything and everyone! All this in an attempt to try and persuade someone to be interested in a little bush clearing called Nebobongo, and all on foot, dusty mile after dusty mile, as the car was being repaired in a garage. Most visits reached a satisfactory issue only after about five tries. Persistence and grace were essential! At last we had lots of promises, some letters, and a truck (borrowed from the Government!) full of blankets, bowls, buckets, thermometers and drugs, and we were all set to go home. While filling up our van at a local pump, I had my briefcase seized from the front seat of my car, with passport, driving licence, identity card, and all my papers.

The British Consul, Mr McGurk, could not have done more for me. He knew all the right people to see, and the right things to do and say, and within ten days I had a new passport (flown up from Leopoldville, with cabled permission from England), new car papers and permits, new medical certificates all signed, and almost all at someone else's most generous expense. Truly people were deeply kind to me, not least the delightful BMS family I stayed with, Mr and Mrs Saunders and their young son, who gave up his bedroom to me for my prolonged four-week visit.

At last, very encouraged, we reached Nebobongo to receive a grand welcome home. The boys' examinations followed. Then came the Independence Day celebrations. Two days later, a little lad, Timothy, the son of one of our church evangelists, was taken desperately ill. I had him in my home so as to be able to give him the very best possible attention, including night nursing care, and the next day we realized he had smallpox. We had eight cases in all. Timothy died the following Saturday. The father and I buried the child at midnight, alone in drizzling rain, to avoid every possible chance of infection. All the contacts were isolated in my home. It was a deeply anxious ten days. We vaccinated, in all, some 80,000 people in the area. There were some fantastic reactions to vaccine, ulcers right down to the bone, awful sloughing, high fevers, and three more patients died. At last, it was over. There were no further cases. The whole station had been bound over in strict isolation and quarantine. They responded wonderfully. One letter had gone out, the first day, duly stoved and disinfected, to seek prayer from home. When she received it, my mother had rung the convent where my sister lived and the community bore us up all through that week, day and night, and God stayed the hand of the epidemic.

Very exhausted, never having properly recovered from the illness of the previous year, I was given permission to go away for six weeks for a complete break, out of the tropical steamy heat of Congo, out of the political unrest and constant threats and fear. I had a wonderful rest and returned very much refreshed. When I arrived back in Paulis by plane I was met and driven home to Nebobongo. There I received such a welcome you would have thought I had been away for a year, not just six weeks!

Storm-clouds were now gathering in the church. Before Independence, all Europeans were invited to all church meetings and were on all committees. Now things were changing. There were tensions. There was a growing consciousness that the Africans did not wholly trust us whites, afraid that we were not really willing to give them absolute equality, absolute authority. They wanted to have their Independence in the church just as others had it in political matters. They wanted Africans to be in charge in every department, including the handling of the finances. The problems were very similar to those of adolescents all over the world. The desire to stand on one's own feet, and not be eternally tied to mother's apron-strings is only natural. So the missionaries were no longer invited to church meetings. Sometimes they were not represented on councils or committees. Decisions were made in the church with no reference to the Europeans or their opinions.

Affairs seemed to come to a head at Christmas 1962 over church finance. There was a good deal of heat in the church meetings and not a little bitterness. Above all, there was this tragic lack of confidence between Africans and Europeans. One day two of the pastors and two schoolmasters came in for coffee, obviously very full, as it were, of the recent troubles. I stood a book on the table between us and asked them if they from their side photographed the book, and at the same moment I took a picture from my side, and then the two films were processed, would they say that my camera lied because it saw the opposite side of the book with a row of black faces behind it, so different from their photograph of the front of the book with a white face behind it. They saw the point, and we had prayer together and yearned that He would help us all through this difficult period of growing-pains.

Then came an unfortunate occurrence. In the summer, we had a young man named Gabriel Mangeyi brought to the hospital with tuberculosis. We knew him well, as he had been a student nurse at Nebobongo years before, but had been dismissed for adultery. He was now married to a woman well known as a harlot. His mother came with him to nurse him, but I forbad the wife to come to the hospital, trying to protect the twenty or more student male nurses from her evil influence. However, she came, and after three nights, Gabriel's mother came to tell me that this woman had sinned with the son of my evangelist Agoya.

The case was taken to the church, amidst much heart anguish. Throughout it all Stephen, their son, repeatedly denied the accusation of Gabriel's mother. But the council decided that Agoya and Taadi would have to leave us to take over a small village church, so that their wayward son could go with them to be under their direct discipline. For various reasons, however, action on their decision had to be postponed. Taadi was ill, and also expecting another little one. Also the church had no evangelist whom they could send immediately to replace Agoya. So several months passed without the sentence being implemented.

Thus it was that Agoya and his family were still at Nebobongo when we heard that Gabriel had been brought to repentance at a church conference and had confessed that the whole story had been a lie, to 'get even' with Agoya who had been responsible for his dismissal years earlier. My heart lurched badly. I felt I never wanted to see Gabriel, his wife or mother again after such evil.

On Boxing Day, this mother came to see me at Nebobongo to say that she wanted my forgiveness. 'What for?' I asked. 'I don't know', she replied; 'but the church says I cannot take my Christmas Communion while I have anything in my heart against you.' I felt anger well up in my heart. What deceit! To say she didn't know what she had done or for what she sought forgiveness. She went on her knees to me, and in a moment, I struck her, pulling her to her feet and demanding that she never kneel to me, but only to the Lord. Stunned she left me, and miserably I turned and entered the house. I had lost my temper, I had struck an African. After an hour's fighting with myself, I went out, got into the van, and set off for Ibambi to take the matter to the church council. On the way, I overtook the woman walking back to Ibambi and gave her a lift. It was not the easiest of journeys!

Arrived at Ibambi, I went straight to the house where the African church elders were meeting, told them exactly what had happened, and asked them to mediate between us. They were amazed. Apparently this was the first time that a European had taken a case to the Africans and not to the other missionaries. They heard the case, African fashion, and eventually we both sought forgiveness and shook hands. Next day, the two pastors came to see me at Nebobongo. Very humbly they confessed that it was jealousy that had caused them to insist that Agoya and Taadi should leave Nebobongo because I thought so much of them. Now they wanted our forgiveness and to assure them and myself that the church had agreed that they both should stay with me. And so that day yet deeper and closer links were forged between my heart and theirs as they acknowledged that I was indeed one of themselves. Humbly, I realized that God was blessing us through it all, and teaching us to walk together in close fellowship without the barriers of pride and race.

National events were moving fast. Thieving was rife. It was hard, if not impossible, to get justice. Jealousies and suspicions were on the increase. Every man was afraid of his neighbour lest he lose his job through false accusations, and no man lightly agreed to help a European lest he lose his job through being thought to fraternize or encourage neo-colonialism. John and Del Gunningham, fellow-missionaries from the north-west of our Province, joined us for her confinement, and he did a wonderful job putting a new permanent roof on the other missionaries' house on the station. Whilst they were with us we had a visit from the Inspector of Medical Schools from Leopoldville quite unexpectedly, and Del did wonders in catering for everyone! Then the local chiefs sent us men to build new wards, an out-patients' block, and a new primary school for the children. The station was a noisy hive of activity for many weeks. The building programme was not without incident, grumbling and strikes, but we managed to steer through without too bad a break, and eventually everything was completed.

Christmas 1963 came and went without undue incident. But early in 1964 we began to hear rumours and odd scraps of news of troubles down in the south of Congo, including rioting, looting, and burning of villages. Unrest in our area increased. Shortages were more acute, prices were spiralling, and wages kept going up and up. Tensions between Africans and Europeans were no longer hidden.

As before, this was reflected in the church. The devil seemed to be fighting hard to destroy the work of years. Misunderstandings were rife; seeds of bitterness were sown in many hearts; feelings of distrust grew between different groups. Yet through it all God most graciously continued to bless the ministry of the gospel and many souls were added to the church. Through the four years since Independence we had taken a chapter a day from Scripture in our morning Bible School at Nebobongo, starting from Genesis, with a synopsis and analysis of each book as we commenced and finished it. The elders had followed right through the course, with detailed notes, forming each one his own commentary in Swahili. And now we were nearing the end. On Saturdays we had had classes for studying the doctrines of the Christian faith and always these were amazingly well attended. The choir was an active integral part of our church life, and the eighty members sang a Swahili translation of Handel's 'Unto us a Child is born' from *Messiah* at the Easter conference, with no orchestral accompaniment other than the birds. They had learnt it to a tuning fork, line by line, in tonic sol-fa!

During the year, various projects began to come to fruition after years of praying. A branch of the Evangelical Alliance had been formed, uniting all the six Protestant Missionary Societies working in the north-east Congo. This was the corner-stone of the foundation of an Inter-Mission educational programme for creating one united full-grade secondary school, to prepare our Mission-trained youngsters for University entrance so that we might have keen spiritual men in the future government of Congo. There was also an Inter-Mission Medical programme for creating one central hospital, sufficiently well built and equipped to be passed by the Government as a training school for African paramedical and nursing personnel. These were thrilling days, and I was very privileged to represent our Mission at several of these Inter-Mission conferences discussing these programmes.

Then in July 1964, we had our triennial field conference, attended by all the missionaries and by two representatives from each African church council in the area. About twenty-four of us, and nearly sixty of them, met for a week of prayer and fellowship, and to discuss placing of personnel and projects for the coming three years. It was a blessed week, and many of us felt that God was very specially present in our midst, breaking down barriers, bringing us back to each other in a fuller unity and trust, and dispersing us afterwards with a renewed vision and purpose.

As we looked back during the months of travail that followed, we were always so grateful to God that He allowed us that week of united fellowship. We did not then know that it would be the last time that many of us would ever meet in that manner. Within six months, four of our missionaries were to be murdered, and all of us driven from the country. But our last memories were to be of the joy and happiness and unity of church and Mission together.

# 11

# Nearly Exhausted

Throughout the years since Independence, there had been a strange spiritual battle in my own heart. Often an apparent darkness and loneliness hedged me in, yet always there was the complete certainty of being in the centre of His will; often I lacked any consciousness of His presence and knew no burden in prayer, yet always there was quiet confidence of being a 'vessel only'. I had a growing hunger after Him, and a deepening realization of the wonderful process of identification with Christ for the Africans I was trying to win. 'Christ in you, the hope of glory' was the phrase often in my mind. He was working out His love for them through me. Every act of service was a manifestation of His love.

The church of Jesus Christ in Congo seemed to be going through a process of adolescence, and there were many growing pains. For fifty years the missionaries had been working in the area, preaching the gospel and training the early church, much as a parent does a child, with a somewhat similar relationship, one of paternalism. Now the child, fully grown, becoming yearly more educated and sophisticated, learning of other lands through radio and travelling, was demanding her independence, unwilling for the close parental discipline any longer, fighting to break free, determined to show that she could stand by herself.

There were many tensions. Some missionaries felt that the church was ungrateful for the years of sacrificial love, and that they were no longer wanted. Yet they were sure that the church was not yet ready for them to leave. The Africans felt that the missionaries did not trust them, that they always wanted to 'boss', to be in charge, to tell them what to do and how to do it. The problem was particularly acute in the matter of church collections and other general administrative decisions. The Africans broke loose. They held their own meetings, dispersed their own finances, and asked advice of no-one. The 'parent' was hurt. Mistakes were made; finances were in a muddle; debts were incurred. The Africans were proud and would not concede that anything was wrong. They were afraid they might incur the 'told-you-so' attitude. The missionaries began to withhold their offerings, feeling that the funds to which they had been contributing were being mismanaged. The troubles increased and some difficult years ensued.

On top of all this, possibly due to the great strain through which all were passing, there were misunderstandings amongst the missionaries themselves. I myself was criticized for siding with Africans against the missionaries, whereas one's aim was to seek Him in each situation and to see Him glorified in each life. There was consequent loneliness, linked with overwork and weariness. At such times I recalled again all He had suffered for me on the cross of Calvary; now it was my privilege to share the suffering for those I was trying to reach. He was made sin for me; how closely was I willing to be identified with Him? With them? Was I prepared to face the cost?

Our Mission motto was deeply burnt into my heart: 'If Jesus Christ be God and died for me, then no sacrifice can be too great for me to make for Him.' This was my firm belief, and I prayed to God that I might be found worthy.

On 7th August 1964, came the outbreak of the rebellion in the north-east province. We were caught absolutely unawares, not having the slightest thought of all that might be involved. I was setting off in the Mission truck to Kampala in Uganda, a thousand miles east, to collect two tons of medical goods and supplies, food and petrol, when the news that Stanleyville had fallen to the hands of the rebels reached us. We waited to see what this would involve. No-one was very perturbed. We had had troubles and riots for the last four years.

Eight days later, on Saturday, 15th August, the soldiers reached us. A truck-load drove into the hospital compound bringing with them a wounded civilian. That was the start of five months of occupation. They were brutal and coarse, rough and domineering. Their language was threatening and obscene. All of us were cowed. We did exactly what they demanded, mostly without argument. We gave them what they asked for without debating the price. Africans carried flowers and shouted the slogans of the day as an act of obedience to the new powers. Rumours poured round us. We heard of murders, brutalities, beatings, stealings, looting and burning. We did not wish to be involved, so we obeyed. We heard that the rebel army had taken first Wamba, and then Paulis, with very little resistance. Some said that the streets ran with blood, that they had to walk with care not to step on a corpse. All the previous leaders, all those who had been in Government pay, were being systematically liquidated. They were searched out, evilly treated, and ultimately brutally murdered. Cars and trucks in the area were commandeered. To hear a vehicle on the road was synonymous with the approach of the army. Whenever they came to the village they brought a terrible sense of fear, a presence of evil and wickedness. And they were for ever passing, passing. Would they enter? What ought we to do?

Thus began the war of nerves. We had rebels amongst the patients, especially in the men's ward, and I felt they could well be spying on us. Care was necessary in every word we spoke. The soldiers came to visit friends day and night, but one never knew when they drove on to the compound for what they had come. Many times they told us in those first weeks that this war had nothing to do with us Europeans. It was a party-political, civil war. They had nothing against us as whites, and especially as Protestant missionaries. They wanted us to stay and continue with our task. When the New Order was established, they would recognize our good work officially and do all they could to obtain the supplies we needed. But in almost the same breath they would threaten us that, if we meddled with politics, if we interfered with their method of administering justice, if we helped any 'wanted' man to hide in the hospital, then we should be treated as traitors and shot. And the hospital would be burnt to the ground. It was not easy to keep calm in such an atmosphere.

Suffering? Yes; it began early on. The mental suffering of uncertainty, not knowing quite what they would do, nor when. At Nebobongo we were virtually cut off from the rest of the Mission since we were not allowed to travel. And we were completely cut off from the outside world, for there was no mail or radio communication with anyone outside the Province. There was no way of letting anyone know how we were. At first we all thought it would speedily be over, one way or the other, and that we should be allowed to continue our work under the former or latter Government. Then things began to drag. We saw truckloads of young teenagers passing along the road and were told that they were conscripts going to the front to fight. We never saw any coming back. We saw a van go by full of European nuns and priests. Later it returned. Where had it been and why? We feared for them and what they were being made to suffer. We heard that the local chief had been caught, bound and beaten; then he was taken to the people's tribunal at Wamba, found guilty, flayed alive and eaten. No wonder we did not sleep well. No wonder we were not hungry.

Suffering? Yes; in fear for our own people. One of our girl nurses was assaulted. Two of the women were taken from the maternity compound, rudely flung on to a truck and driven off. They threatened to take two of our little girls to 'serve' the soldiers. Primary school children were being rounded up in other areas as army conscripts. Would they come and do the same here? They inspected our homes, searching for transistor radios and tape-recorders, threatening death should they find any. I had none; but would they go and search the other home where both the missionaries had them? They demanded food, and clothing, and spectacles. I gave what I had. Then came the time when there was nothing to give, and they raised their rifles to strike me as a liar, and I feared for the physical pain. A male nurse, away on holiday, made his way back to us through the forest, telling of being hunted for ten days, his father having been murdered, his home burnt and looted, and his mother dying of heart failure. We were one with them, identified with them in their suffering, and our hearts bled with theirs.

Suffering? Yes; the day when they turned against us whites. News was seeping through that the National Army was employing white troops, mercenary soldiers from South Africa and other lands, and that the rebel army was being turned back. Rebel soldiers were being killed despite the witchcraft and the promises made at their initiation rights. It must be that the white man was using a more powerful witchcraft, possibly emanating from the white people in the area. Therefore we were to be bound and herded together, possibly shot. They were brutal and drunken. They cursed and swore, they struck and kicked, they used the butt-end of rifles and rubber truncheons. We were roughly taken, thrown in prisons, humiliated, threatened. We were driven forty miles north to be shot-but God intervened and we were driven home again! The whole church had been praying ceaselessly for our deliverance. We were four weeks under house-arrest, four weeks filled with petty interferences and pilferings, endless threatenings and uncertainties. The Christians rallied round wonderfully to help us and out of their poverty poured on us gifts of chickens and eggs, rice and peanuts. Each time a truck-load of soldiers arrived they were always there beside us, to protect us and encourage us.

Suffering? Yes; impossible though it seemed, the situation got worse. We were taken away from our dear Africans and placed under close guard, under prison conditions, in the Roman Catholic convent at Wamba. We saw the nuns wickedly treated, beaten and humiliated. We were completely at their mercy, and yet strangely God moved upon them to protect us, and also to feed us. Rumours fed our fears, and each long day led into a long night of waiting, hoping, expectant for deliverance the following dawn, but only to meet with disappointment—and to start again.

We heard that our stations had been utterly ransacked and destroyed, and we longed for news of our Africans. Were they suffering for having befriended us? We felt we were always being watched and had to take extra care of all that was said and done.

Then came Christmas Day, and with it the next move. The soldiers began taking us group by group, in a small open van, a hundred miles east. The idea, apparently, was to keep us with the retreating army as front-line hostages. The group I was with was taken on the Sunday, but after travelling only seventy-five miles, we were put off at a house in the jungle—nineteen defenceless women and children surrounded by some seventy-five men, soldiers and others, all filled with hatred and evil intentions towards us. Food was scarce; water almost unprocurable. Danger was imminent; fear was in the very air we breathed. Wickedness surrounded us on all sides; it seemed inevitable that we should be killed. And in my heart was an amazing peace, a realization that I was being highly privileged to be identified with Him in a new way, in the way of Calvary.

I witnessed the outpouring of hatred against the white man. I became very conscious of the extent to which we had earned this. If I was willing to be identified as a European with the sin of the white people against the African in the past fifty or more years—the injustices, the cruelties, the hardships, cheap labour with flogging, black women-folk and illegitimate children, bribery and corruption in courts and administration—then perhaps, in some small way, I was privileged to be part of the extirpation of that sin. We whites had to be identified with it, to bear its penalty, to suffer for it, that Africa might be rid of it, to start again freed of it. This was our hope; this was what made it worth while. Somehow He was working out His purposes for our Congo; somehow He would bring ultimate blessing out of the terror of all this suffering; for He alone could make even the wrath of man to praise Him.

Now the end seemed very near. We were expecting death at any moment. The guards were becoming more and more restive. A sense of oppression was closing in on us. Suddenly there was a distant noise. Was it friend or foe? Everyone stiffened and listened intently. We were bundled into an inner room, flung on the ground, kicked and beaten. Then the guards retired, locking the door. We heard the distant noise growing; it was machine-gun firing! Hope soared, could it be our deliverers? They mustn't pass us by; they must see a white face somehow; we must show them we were there. Would our guards fire on us through the window? Nothing seemed to matter any longer except the thought of deliverance. I threw myself forward towards the window. There were jeeps, trucks, men, noise, shouting, firing. Someone was kicking at the door. Women were crying, children were sobbing. The door gave, and a white man burst through to us. The room seemed to fill with white soldiers.

'It's all over; don't cry, mother. Yes, yes, we'll take you all. No hurry; take your time. We can't take any luggage, I'm afraid, as we're a bit full up.'

So their chatter soothed through our tumultuous thoughts. We were safe! It was all over. We were still alive. The terrible nightmare was over.

# 12

# Gloriously Worth It!

Home! It was less than three days from the moment of deliverance, but it was hard to believe it. The mercenary soldiers had been kindness itself. That Wednesday evening we were taken to their barracks in the Paulis brewery, all ten of us Protestant missionaries together, united at last with our two menfolk. They carried up jugs of hot water for us to have the first proper wash for many weeks. They served us a lovely hot meal which we could eat in peace, not fearfully glancing round in case of trouble. They brought us mattresses and blankets to sleep in comfort on the floor of their large sitting-room. Next day, they showed us all over the site, chatted with us, photographed us, and at last waved us farewell as we left in a great American transport plane along with 125 other refugees.

At Leopoldville we were given a tremendous and moving welcome by the missionaries there who had been anxiously praying for us and waiting for us over the months. On New Year's Day everyone helped us, to get clothes, to arrange passports and papers, to book seats on a flight to Amsterdam. That evening we were again in the air, flying towards Europe—from 90° to snow! At each stop on the route friends known and unknown seemed to vie with each other in giving help and showing consideration, especially at Amsterdam where we changed planes for the final flight for London.

Through a battery of television and newspaper cameras, to the customs sheds, and straight to a telephone booth. Excitedly I put in a reverse charge call—I hadn't a penny in the world—and there was dear Mother's voice. What a moment!

That evening I was home. The long five months of nightmare were over. But it was not immediately easy to wake up and realize that we were still alive. We had lived facing and expecting death for too long to accept easily the fact of life again. Family, friends, newspaper reporters, church, letters, flowers—it was an overwhelming welcome, as to one back from the dead. At hospital, where we went for general medical check-ups as soon as an appointment could be made, we were all given every kindliness and consideration, and were each recommended to take a fairly long spell of quiet convalescence. For me, it was nearly ten weeks before I really snapped out of the stupor and daze, back to reality, and began to realize once more that life had present-tense claims and that there was still plenty to be done!

After a lovely four-week holiday with my mother and sister down in Cornwall, mainly sleeping, eating, reading and resting, I felt reorientated, for He enabled me to look back on it all and to see it was a great privilege, offered to me from His nail-pierced hands, gloriously worthwhile in His perfect economy. There followed six months of deputation touring, which took me all over the British Isles and twice to the continent, speaking at some two hundred meetings, telling of the great and all-sufficient grace of Jesus Christ, and urging people to accept the burden of believing prayer for our Congolese church.

We knew nothing of their needs at that time. Had they suffered reprisals for our deliverance? We longed over them, travailing again that Christ might be formed in them. It was a glorious tour. My desire was to present a positive message of His redeeming love, of the greatness of Calvary, the privilege of suffering with Him, the realization in a new way of His pre-eminence. As I told the story of His dealings with me to His praise and glory, my heart became fully comforted and in tune to accept all the suffering as from Him. The wounds were healed. The mental shock was alleviated. Slowly He filled me again with a great joy and wonder at His precious goodness.

Then in August a thrilling day arrived, bringing our first letters from our Nebobongo family. The National Army had at last reached them and delivered them from the long ten months of rebel occupation. The first, dated 6th June, was filled with praise to God for His goodness to them and to us in keeping us all safe. They told of all the rumours they had heard of our fate, of their fears for our safety, and of their great joy for us when they received our letters from the hands of the delivering soldiers of the National Army as they arrived on 5th June. These had taken five months to travel forty-five miles!

A group of the faithfuls had stayed at each of our stations, guarding the property as best they could and watching and praying daily to see how the Lord would overrule. In April, however, the rebel soldiers had made Ibambi their headquarters, taking over all the houses and everything they could find, hoisting their flag, and ordering the remaining Africans to serve them as house-boys. Some managed to get away, with nothing but the clothes they wore and their Bibles in their hands. They lost everything just as we had. 'We are now as we were when you first came to Congo fifty years ago', they wrote. The rebels had declared that on 15th June they would kill all the evangelists. But on 5th June the delivering National Army walked in! Everyone had fled to the jungle for fear at the approach of the army and troops, but were soon persuaded to come back to the station. What a day of praise followed! The great church at Ibambi was filled to overflowing as crowd after crowd gave thanks to God for their deliverance. 'All the church monies have been taken; all the chairs, tables, etc., destroyed. But we have one piece of wealth left—our salvation. How we thank and praise God that He sent you to us to give us the only true wealth, that no man can take from us, that cannot be destroyed, the truth as it is in Scripture, our Lord and Saviour Jesus Christ. Hallelujah!'

Letters began getting through to us, week by week, and all were similarly full of praise and joy, and ended with a plea to us to return to help them and to have fellowship with them again as soon as it was safe and possible to do so. Our hearts were stirred. There were no grumbles, no bitterness, just praise. And the sense of their need was overwhelming. Two and a half million Congolese in the north-east province without one single doctor, black or white, with no secondary school teachers, their shops empty, no grain for planting, without clothes, food or medicine. At once, we put in our applications to go back just as soon as it was considered reasonable by the powers that be. I continued deputation with renewed vigour and refreshed vision, telling of their need for our prayers, and for further personnel for the tremendous task of re-establishing all the church services they were so sorely in need of spiritual, medical, educational. Two months in a post-graduate course followed, preparing one's mind for the task ahead, and letters went to and fro. A new programme was slowly emerging in our hearts to meet the new day of opportunity as well as the urgent needs of the hour.

Our Africans, both the local Christians and those in local government, want us back to work alongside them, as brothers and fellow-labourers. But it will be, it must be, a new relationship, that of adults of maturity. No-one who has been through such sufferings can come out the same as before. I believe we have been welded into one as never before. The tensions and suspicions between African and European have been destroyed; and we must see to it that they are never restored.

At Christmas 1965 we had a wonderful family reunion, the first for seventeen years! My brother and his wife, my three sisters and their husbands, together with seven nieces and nephews were all gathered together, and it certainly was a great day. It was just one more climax to this amazing year, as each one could look back and praise God for His infinite goodness and preserving care in so many different ways. It was also the occasion for saying farewell, as I set my face to prepare for returning to the land of my adoption. Making lists, shopping, packing, labelling; visits to shipping agents, consular offices, and to doctor and dentist; arrangements with bank manager and with income tax offices. Then came the final meetings and farewells, the letters and reports. But above all, there was the joy of planning for, and purchase and construction of a fully equipped mobile hospital. This is a long-wheelbase Land Rover, with its overweight springs and four-wheel drive to stand up to our impossible roads, fitted and equipped with a small laboratory, pharmacy, dispensary and everything needed for major emergency surgery, and convertible into a caravan at night, with electric light and air-conditioning! A long-cherished dream is at last seeing the light of day, provided by the generosity of Christians, stirred to give to help the Congolese in their need, through the many deputation meetings. Surely He has seen fit to give it to us 'for such a day as this'.

11th of March 1966. What a day of joy; the day we sail for Congo, back to our beloved African fellow-workers, to take up the task again that He has committed to our hands. We go back at a time of unprecedented needs. In our northeastern Province, with its two and a half million Congolese, there is a strong, virile, active church, with her own pastors and elders. But they ask us to join them to help in the vast task of education—primary, secondary, technical, medical, and theological—at a time when they have only a handful of Africans trained for teaching in senior primary schools, a hundred or so for junior primary, but none for the senior schools. There is the essential need of aid for their medical programme, for they have no doctors, less than a handful of fully qualified nurses, and only a hundred or so assistant nurses, scattered in badly damaged, poorly equipped, rural dispensaries, with no medicines, no supervision, and the constant threat of the outbreak of serious epidemics. They look to us also for help in organizing youth work and training the new generation to take its place in the world with respect and not shame, with courage and not constant fear, with honour in the place of bribery and corruption. They need men and women to help with the printing of good literature, with its writing, translation and distribution; to help with the establishment of a theological college for the training of pastors to lead the young church, men who will take their place as teachers in the different area Bible schools for training their own evangelists. Possibilities abound on every side. The doors are wide open. The invitation has been issued to all who have seen the vision, and heard the call of the risen Lord, to those who know the joy of the mystery, 'Christ in you, the hope of glory.' Surely indeed in the coming years, we are going to see 'the valley of Achor' become 'a door of hope'.

# Epilogue

I have used some of the three weeks which it takes from London to Mombasa to put the finishing touches to this story of God's dealings with me. As I have read the chapters again, it is clear that certain landmarks stand out very clearly. There are lessons which I had to learn and warnings which I still need to heed.

First, I would put the realization that in myself I was a failure. I was unable to reach the standard I myself had set, let alone God's. Try as I would, I met only frustration in this longing to achieve, to be worthy. I'm sure that, for me, this first lesson had to be thoroughly learnt so that, when I did come to acknowledge God as my Lord and Master, I might not succumb again to the temptation to feel that I could succeed or achieve anything ultimately worthwhile in my own strength.

Secondly, I had to learn that, of myself, I could be ashamed of sin and hate its consequences, but that I could not actually hate the sin itself. On the contrary, I found pleasure in it. I despised myself for enjoying what I knew I ought to hate, but I continued to enjoy it nevertheless. Like Paul, who describes what seems to have been a similar experience in Romans 7, my position was, 'I do not do the good I want, but the evil I do not want is what I do.' Now hatred of sin is a gift of the Holy Spirit. After trying hard to make myself hate what I knew I enjoyed, and nearly despairing in the effort, I came at last to the limit by asking God 'to make me willing to be made willing to hate what He hated', and He graciously did for me what I asked.

Then I had to learn that there are some glorious views en route, as well as many pleasant valleys, that do not necessarily help in the upward climb. Certain experiences came and entered my life. They could have grown big and all-important, but when measured against the course of the journey they were non-essential to the main progress. Again, other incidents were eventually found to be of passing interest only. But they might have seriously hampered the journey if carried along as an important item. I gladly accepted and entered into each experience as God graciously bestowed it, but I had to learn to cling to Him, my Guide, and not to the various feelings stirred by the passing views.

Then those wise words of Elizabeth at Mission Head-quarters in my 131 training days have remained with me through the following years as a beacon on the path. 'If you're doing it for me (or for any man) you may as well go home...You're doing it for the Lord and He saw the first time you cleaned it...' The day all our midwives had to be dismissed and the maternity compound closed, I asked myself, how had I failed them? Where had we gone wrong? Recriminations, accusations crowded into my mind. What will the Mission say? Or the church? This was fear of man. 'You are doing this work for Me, and I have seen all you have poured in, of heart and soul; I know.' So He breathed peace into my striving heart—the same old message, but ever new.

Another deep truth I have learnt, and one we can all cling to, is that God is personally interested in us as individuals and that He will engineer our circumstances and daily lives so that He can thereby make us like Jesus. This takes the sting out of much that could otherwise hurt. He allows various accidents and happenings to occur, which will affect us deeply, perhaps, only so that, through them, we may be drawn closer to Himself.

There were the times of deep humiliation, coupled with a sense of insufficiency, both as a doctor and as a missionary. Here, too, these negative experiences were allowed to reveal positive truth. Only as I found my own insufficiency did I realize His sufficiency. Such ability as I had to lead, to organize, to administer, all tended to strengthen my personal ego and pride. This was true also of my popularity with the Africans and the respect I received from the Government. My pride was big enough already! It was a stalwart prop on which I leant for self-encouragement to continue and to stick the job. God had to take the prop away, and I did not like it—until I found that He was there, willing to fill my every need and to give all the encouragement I desired! Even my inverted pride in my inabilities had to be dealt with. I said I could not operate. I had not been trained and I was scared stiff. I just wasn't willing to trust the Lord to work this out. I did not want Him to make me willing to operate; I wanted to go on not wanting to! But when during the first six months of Independence He allowed every surgeon in the area to leave, I just had to operate. Then He showed that He was able to undertake for this need also as I was willing to be made willing. My pride in my inability had been as great a prop in my self-preservation as my pride in my abilities was to my self-realization. Both had to be taken away that I might learn that Christ wanted the pre-eminence in every department of my life.

In the Introduction, I mentioned the importance of distinguishing between the slight going down from a peak experience in order to set out across the valley to climb another higher peak, and the real going down of returning to base. The former may appear to be a stretch of the journey in shadows, but the latter would have been acknowledgement of defeat and failure. For many years, I did not discern this difference, and thereby suffered many long heartaches unnecessarily, listening to the devil's accusations instead of the Spirit's counsel.

Another clear truth that has come out so forcibly into the sunlight through the last few chapters is that God has no second-best. This is very often a contradiction of terms. If I am in God's will for me, it is His very best for me. God is eternal present tense. If I step out of His will, then I deliberately choose my own path and I have nothing of His best. When I confess my error, seek His loving forgiveness, and return to His will, then at once He restores me. It is always present to Him, so at the moment of restoration I am in His present will for me. Once repentance is real, and forgiveness sought, the past is past, and has no longer an interpretation in the present. The present may well be different from the 'might-have-been', it may well be affected by the consequences of previous disobedience and sin which can leave their mark on both character and circumstance, but nevertheless, it is the best in the immediate now. I have found this to be a most liberating and glorious truth. If it were not so, who among us would not live his life in an atmosphere of continual regret?

The night I was first taken captive by the rebel soldiers He worked that liberation for me in the midst of all the horror and anguish! I saw it in a verse in Peter's Epistle: 'For what glory is it, if, when ye be buffeted for your faults, ye shall take it patiently? but if, when ye do well, and suffer for it, ye take it patiently, this is acceptable with God' (1 Peter 2:20). In that moment, I knew utterly and unquestioningly, whatever the past might have held of failures, that I was in the second half of the verse. God allowed the circumstances to be such that even I, so often a veritable 'doubting Thomas', could not argue. Therefore He showed me, with a gentle smile, a smile of reproof perhaps, that I had taken so long to learn, a smile of deep love that I truly wanted to learn, that I was 'acceptable with God', and this could only mean that I was in the centre of His will. Certainly this could be no 'second-best'.

The last months of 1964 brought to a culmination so much of all He had been teaching me through the years. The suffering just seemed to highlight His love. I have summarized in my own heart the specific lessons of my months in captivity to help me not to lose anything of their wonder and their worth.

1. Participation in His suffering is necessary to each one if we are to fulfil His will in this world;
2. The pre-eminence of His Son is essential that we may know in very truth His all-sufficiency at all times;
3. Praise through His sacrifice is possible even in the midst of danger and horror, as we rejoice in His working out His purposes.

Above all, I have learnt a little of the tremendous privilege of walking with Him, of being identified with Him. Christ not only bore my sin; He was made sin for me. He identified Himself utterly with us sinners that He might redeem us. Now if He should seek a body, a vessel, in whom to live, that He might identify Himself with the deepest needs and hungers of Congolese hearts, was I willing to be this vessel? More than willing! I entered into the great privilege of bearing about the One who had paid the supreme cost.

'Brethren, I count not myself to have apprehended: but this one thing I do, forgetting those things which are behind, and reaching forth unto those things which are before, I press toward the mark for the prize of the high calling of God in Christ Jesus' (Phil. 3:13-14).

# About the Author

Dr Helen Roseveare (1925-2016) went to the Congo as a missionary between 1953 and 1973. A pioneer of vital medical work in the rainforests of this region, she had a major impact long after she left. Through many trials, she lived out her life striving to serve her Lord with every day – and encouraging those around her to do the same.

Some of her works include:

*Digging Ditches: The Latest Chapter of an Inspirational Life*
(ISBN 978-1-84550-058-0)

*Give Me This Mountain*
(ISBN 978-1-84550-189-1)

*He Gave Us a Valley*
(ISBN 978-1-84550-190-7)

*Living Faith: Willing to be Stirred as a Pot of Paint*
(ISBN 978-1-84550-295-9)

*Living Fellowship: Willing to be the Third side of the Triangle*
(ISBN 978-1-84550-351-2)

*Living Holiness: Willing to be the Legs of a Galloping Horse*
(ISBN 978-1-84550-352-9)

*Living Sacrifice: Willing to be Whittled as an Arrow*
(ISBN 978-1-84550-294-2)